THE HARMAN FAMILY'S LUNDY
1925-1969

Martin Coles Harman (1885-1954). Photograph taken in 1928

THE HARMAN FAMILY'S LUNDY
1925-1969

by

Members of the
Lundy Field Society

First published 2013
to mark a notable birthday

www.lundy.org.uk

Design and layout by André Coutanche

Printed by Short Run Press, Exeter

This publication should be cited as: Members of the Lundy Field Society. 2013.
The Harman Family's Lundy 1925-1969. Lundy Field Society. 144 pp.

ISBN 978-0-9530532-4-7

Foreword

EVERY OWNER has made his mark on Lundy. The de Mariscos of the thirteenth century built their own stronghold (in what is now Bulls Paradise) and were indirectly responsible for the building of the Castle when Henry III took Lundy back from them. The Victorian-era Heaven family left Lundy with both Millcombe House and arguably its most extraordinary building, the Church, and – again indirectly – were the reason the quarry buildings and structures are here today.

What remains from the Harman era lies not so much in the buildings but in the careful conservation of the island's special qualities that have led to its present status as a Site of Special Scientific Interest, and its unspoiled charm. It was Martin Coles Harman's purpose that Lundy should be 'a haven of peace and natural beauty'.

This book is offered by the Lundy Field Society – itself an enduring legacy of the Harman era – in celebration of that ownership, and as a tribute to mark a special birthday of Diana Keast (née Harman), the last member of the family to have been a part-owner of the island. She is a Vice-President of the Society, and so continues her interest and support for the island. She is a very regular visitor to Lundy, where she receives a warm and appreciative welcome, takes a lively interest in events and people, and is a friend to all. Many of the photographs in this book come from Diana's family archives and are published here for the first time. Diana has also contributed memories and anecdotes which enliven the story (look out for the quotes in the blue boxes!).

I recall going to Lundy on one of the paddle steamers as a child and on board was a revered gentleman – it turned out to be Albion Harman – who was taking something over to the island in a cage covered in a blanket. Enquiries from curious children led to the blanket being pulled back to reveal dark-coloured rabbits!

Although my active involvement with Lundy started at about the time that the Harman family passed on ownership to the National Trust, the legacy left by those earlier years was a part of what I became familiar with during my stays on the island. In recent years, my knowledge of the island has been enriched by the memories that Diana Keast so freely makes available to those who are lucky enough to be in her company. Thank you, Diana - this book is for you.

Keith Hiscock
Chairman, Lundy Field Society
January, 2013

Introduction and thanks

THIS BOOK does not attempt to be a definitive history of Lundy during the ownership of the Harman family. Other works cover Lundy in this period in a more formal way, most recently Myrtle Ternstrom's *The Lords of Lundy*, while Felix Gade's memoirs, *My Life on Lundy*, are required reading for anyone wanting to know about this time. The intention here is to tell some of the stories of the period, some well known and others much less so, and to illustrate them with a wide range of contemporary photographs and other material, much of which has not been published before.

Still less is this a history of the Harman family itself during that time. Individuals appear in these pages as part of the stories we have chosen to tell; there are many more stories for which there hasn't been room, and different stories would focus on different members of the family and islanders. No disrespect is intended to anyone whose full contribution to the life of the island might not be reflected in these pages.

The majority of the photographs in this book are from the collections of Diana Keast and Myrtle Ternstrom. Specific photos have come from Gordon Coward, Roger Davies, R.L. Knight, E. Stanbrooke, Mike Tedstone and James Thomas. Other contributions have come from other people, and thanks are offered to Mr and Mrs Blythe and all who have helped this publication in any way. Special thanks go to the members of the working group who prepared the book: Myrtle Ternstrom, Diana Keast and André Coutanche. Most of the illustrations and all the text are copyright. If any copyright material has been used inadvertently without permission, the Lundy Field Society apologises and would be pleased to be informed.

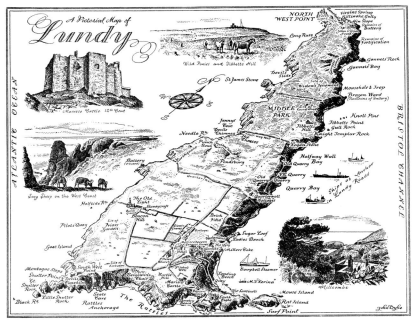

'A Pictorial Map of Lundy', drawn by John Dyke, which appeared in
'Lundy Bristol Channel: An Illustrated Guide' by Rosemary Studdy, published in 1949

Contents

Watercolour of the Lundy Cabbage, painted by Susan Ogilvy, daughter of Colonel Donald Easten, M.C., who was John Pennington Harman's Commanding Officer at Kohima (see page 94). The Lundy Cabbage is endemic to Lundy and it has two endemic species of insect living on it – a unique situation in the U.K. It was first identified during the Harman years by a Braunton doctor, Frederick Elliston Wright, in 1935

A Surrey family

ALTHOUGH THE HARMAN'S ANCESTORS were from Lewes, Sussex, the family home when Martin Coles Harman and his brothers and sisters were growing up was in the village of Chaldon, Surrey. Chaldon is on the North Downs, to the west of Caterham.

This family photograph, so characteristic of Edwardian middle-class prosperity, was taken in 1912 and shows the family on the tennis lawn at Dean's Place, Chaldon, Surrey. Dean's Place (now replaced by four modern houses) was built by 'Grampa Harman' (front, third from left, seated). Martin Coles Harman, his second son, is behind him, standing, and Martin's elder brother, Terry, is standing at the back, third from right. Terry's wife, Isabelle, is seated in front of him with their first baby, also called Martin, on her lap. Isabelle was the sister of Felix Gade, Martin Coles Harman's childhood friend. Felix Gade thus became Martin Coles Harman's brother-in-law, and he subsequently also became his resident agent on Lundy. A simplified family tree, showing some of the members of the family who are mentioned later in this book, appears on page 10.

Martin Coles Harman was frequently known as 'MCH' by his family and friends, and that abbreviation is used throughout this book.

The family had a link with north Devon through MCH's mother, Florence, who came from Parkham, not far from Bideford. A permanent connection was established between Surrey and Lundy later in MCH's life. Martin Coles Harman was very concerned about the threat of urbanisation to Chaldon. He was elected as chairman of the newly established Chaldon Rights of Way Committee in 1920 and the members walked, rode or drove carts along all of the appropriate footpaths and bridle ways in Chaldon. He defended footpaths against the complaints of local land owners and took them to the National Commons and Footpaths Preservation Society which had been founded in 1865. He was successful in the ensuing arbitration.

In 1924 MCH bought 26 acres of land and donated 6½ acres of it to the parish of Chaldon. It is still in use today by the village cricket team. After he had bought Lundy, he had six blocks of the island's granite shipped to Chaldon and placed in the field as a symbol of himself and his five brothers. Named, at his request, 'Six Brothers Field', it was given by MCH to the National Trust in 1926.

The six blocks of granite from Lundy in a corner of Six Brothers Field in Chaldon, Surrey

The National Trust plaque at Six Brothers Field. The deed of gift was dated 31 December 1926 and the date of May 1927 was the formal presentation by the headmaster of Whitgift School (where Martin Coles Harman had been a pupil) to Lord Farrar who received it on behalf of the National Trust

The Harmans of Lundy: a partial family tree

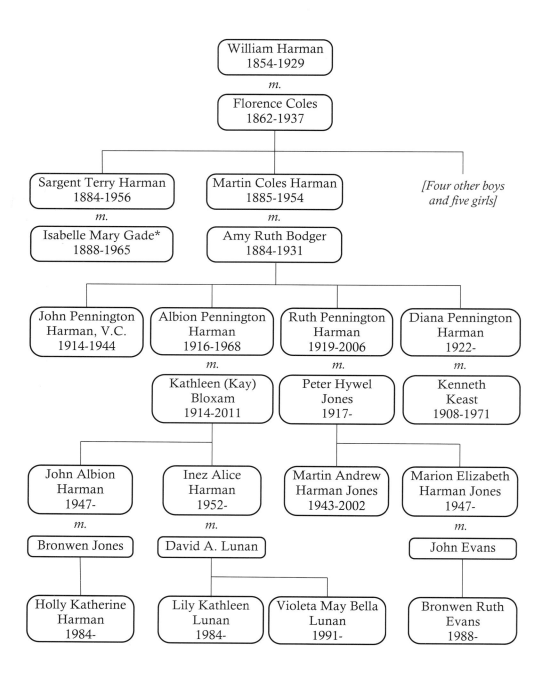

William Harman
1854-1929

m.

Florence Coles
1862-1937

Sargent Terry Harman
1884-1956

m.

Isabelle Mary Gade*
1888-1965

Martin Coles Harman
1885-1954

m.

Amy Ruth Bodger
1884-1931

[Four other boys and five girls]

John Pennington Harman, V.C.
1914-1944

Albion Pennington Harman
1916-1968

m.

Kathleen (Kay) Bloxam
1914-2011

Ruth Pennington Harman
1919-2006

m.

Peter Hywel Jones
1917-

Diana Pennington Harman
1922-

m.

Kenneth Keast
1908-1971

John Albion Harman
1947-

m.

Bronwen Jones

Inez Alice Harman
1952-

m.

David A. Lunan

Martin Andrew Harman Jones
1943-2002

Marion Elizabeth Harman Jones
1947-

m.

John Evans

Holly Katherine Harman
1984-

Lily Kathleen Lunan
1984-

Violeta May Bella Lunan
1991-

Bronwen Ruth Evans
1988-

* Sister of Felix Gade, Martin Coles Harman's agent on Lundy

The first visit – and enchantment

IN 1903 Martin Coles Harman made a day trip in a Bristol Channel pleasure steamer that took him and his friend to Lundy. At the time he was 18 and an office boy in a city company in London, but this visit to Lundy changed his life. He fell in love with the island and said there and then – however unlikely it seemed – that one day he would buy it.

He worked hard and used his outstanding abilities to progress his career, and when the island came up for sale in 1925 he was ready to offer a good price, and Lundy became his. Why?

Martin Coles Harman (right) and his friend, Bert Rockett, on Lundy in 1903

MCH was enchanted by the island. It was set apart, beautiful, peaceful – unspoiled, with a self-contained character of its own. It had not been unduly developed, nor was it a wilderness, but offered a life with a productive farm and fishery, and a range of buildings – not least a delightful modest Georgian-style villa for the lord of the manor, sheltered in the valley of Millcombe, with a beautiful view to the sea in the east. There were no landing facilities, but beaching dinghies on the level and sheltered beach had been the adequate means of landing for centuries. The island was remote and quiet, and it beckoned.

Then there were the birds. The pure air carried their song, and the cliff ledges were crowded with sea birds. To a lover of nature, these, the broad plateau, the magnificent cliffs on the west side, the softer green slopes on the east, presented an idyll far from the City where he spent his working days. What could be better than to take the train from Waterloo to Instow and cross to the island in the *Lerina*; to land in the Bay and rejoice in all he could see?

Beyond all this there was one other major factor that undoubtedly had strong appeal for him: Lundy was believed to be independent. It was not subject to the rules of the mainland authorities, and no income tax or other government levies were paid. This arose from a long tradition – probably when the sums collected could never have exceeded the cost of collection. There were no deeds to validate Lundy's special status, but lawyers for A.L. Christie – from whom MCH subsequently bought Lundy – had established that no taxes were to be paid, the owner of the island was the Governor, and he was entitled to wreck. In fact it could be said that Lundy was regarded in the same way as an independent territory within the British Empire. Harman was a loyal subject of the Crown, but he delighted in Lundy's exceptional status and upheld it with vigour.

This did not mean that he acted as overlord. He was modest and kind, with an original spark of humour. His objectives were always clear: he wanted Lundy to remain a remote, wild and primitive island where wildlife flourished, and all lived in peace and seclusion. The island should be a haven of peace and natural beauty, to be enjoyed by his family and his friends.

The island was his home, and in the early years those visitors who wished to stay were expected to write to him for his agreement, and to introduce themselves on arrival. He was happy to share Lundy with like-minded people who would not require sophisticated arrangements for their comfort, but who would enjoy its simplicity as he did himself

There was one thing about which Martin Coles Harman was adamant: as the name Lundy was thought to be Norse, and to mean 'island of Lund' (however that was interpreted) it would then be tautology to refer to Lundy Island, and so Lundy alone was correct, and was insisted upon.

Dear Mr Britton:

Thank you for your letter of 19th February acknowledging my invitation, and I do hope you will enjoy yourself.

In fact, I feel quite sure that you will, but I beg you to call it "Lundy" and not "Lundy Island" - one ought not to say Lundy Island for the same reason that one ought not to say Anglesey Island, Jersey Island or Guernsey Island. Lunde = puffin, and y = Island, so the word 'island' is redundant. I know a great many people do say Lundy Island, but I want the Field Society to be the centre of light and leading on this subject, if possible. *I hope you don't mind my putting you right on this.*

Yours sincerely,

MARTIN COLES HARMAN

Part of a letter dated 22 February 1949 from Martin Coles Harman to a prospective Lundy Field Society visitor 'putting him right' on what to call the island

Lundy in the 1920s – from the Landing Beach to the Village

W HEN MARTIN COLES HARMAN bought Lundy, the island had been well managed by Augustus Christie as part of his estates, but there was little personal involvement.

For all arrivals, landing was from a dinghy which approached the Landing Beach from the ship which had made the crossing from the mainland. That meant a well-judged jump – timed to miss the wave breaking on shore.

A delicate manoeuvre. Note the large number of vessels at anchor in the Landing Bay

The first thing a visitor in the 1920s might notice was an old cannon lying on the beach, suggestive of its having been thrown down from the castle (the cannon now lies outside the Blacksmith's shed). And perched on a rock to the south of the beach was a fishermen's hut with, nearby, lines for drying the nets. The hut was demolished when the Beach Road was extended to the present Jetty.

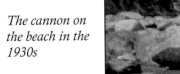

The cannon on the beach in the 1930s

The fishermen's hut on its rock

The South Light, showing the steps which led up to the original entrance

Above that, the path to the South Light zig-zagged up past the fishermen's hut. There was a cable down from the lighthouse that was fixed in the sea, which carried a substantial box, whereby goods could be raised from the Trinity House supply ships. It was forbidden for personnel to travel in the box, unless it were in extreme emergency.

Loading stores by cable to the South Light in the 1950s

On the quay was – and still is – a Trinity House marker stone for 1819, the year that they had built it to help with the landing and haulage of heavy materials for the construction of the Old Light. They also built a store room where heavy goods could be kept until they could be carried up to the lighthouse – although it had also been found necessary to prevent theft of coals etc. Also on the slipway there was a notice carved in stone, stating that the island was entirely private property. It had been placed there by W.H. Heaven when pleasure steamers took to landing trippers without permission on an island that was his home, where there were no rights of way and where there were no facilities for them. Next to this was a limekiln that had formerly been used to burn lime and coal for fertiliser, and beyond that a cave, used for small boats and tackle.

The two stones (above) and the limekiln (left). A landslide in 1954 destroyed both the stone erected by W.H. Heaven and the limekiln. Only the Trinity House stone remains today

Ahead, to the left of the path, in a small clearing, there was a white-painted cottage, Seaview, which was used by the fishermen who came for the fishing season from Sennen, and next to it a black shed for storage and drying nets. From there the original, rough path to the plateau led to the Battlements, where the road curves sharply from Millcombe into St John's Valley.

Seaview (painted white) and the adjacent black shed near the bottom of the Beach Road

At that spot there was a good view of Millcombe Valley with the Villa and, to the left in St John's Valley, the Bungalow. Looking seaward there was a good view of the Bay, the beach, the new slipway, the South Light, and beyond to the North Devon mainland.

The Villa – now Millcombe House – and its walled gardens

The Bungalow, now replaced by Bramble Villa

At the top of the road alongside St John's Valley the path turned to the right, where the church of St Helen dominates the common. It has been variously described as 'magnificent' or 'outrageously out of place'. In the 1920s it was fenced around, with the intention that a parsonage would be provided, and the enclosed land was the property of the Church Commissioners (by gift of H.G. Heaven).

The church as it appeared in the 1920s. The railings demarcated the land owned by the Church of England

Manor Farm Hotel in the early 1920s, before the additional building work which Martin Coles Harman carried out (see page 50). Government House now fills the foreground of this view

Facing east within a walled garden was the Manor Farm Hotel. The path at the back of the hotel led to the refreshment room on the left, originally called the Tent (the Black Shed is now on this site). Beyond that, on the right, was what MCH subsequently re-christened the Marisco Tavern.

'The Stores' – which were also the tavern – before they were named 'The Marisco Tavern' by Martin Coles Harman

Bulls Paradise | Linhay | Shippons (cow sheds) | Barn | Rocket Shed | Tavern Block | Barton Cottages

Pigs Paradise | Refreshment Room | Kitchen Gardens | Pigsties | Blacksmith's Shop | Hotel

This photograph was taken from the Church tower in the 1930s, but it shows the village virtually unchanged from the time when Martin Coles Harman bought Lundy in 1925

> *My first memory of Lundy is mother calling me to listen to the six o'clock news with her on our big 'portable' wireless. We heard 'Mr Martin Coles Harman, the City financier, has bought the island of Lundy ...'. This was November 1925 at home in Sussex.*

Lundy in the 1920s: the Castle

MARTIN COLES HARMAN was particularly interested in the Castle – magnificently situated at the top of the cliff overlooking the Landing Bay. Approaching it as one climbed the Beach Road meant taking the small path to the left at the Battlements, which is thought to be the original way up to the island. This passed Cliff Bungalow (now Hanmers) and crossed the dry moat, to arrive at the busy area of the Signal Station.

Cliff Bungalow before it was extended and renovated to become today's 'Hanmers'

The first thing to catch the eye was the Post Office (now extended as Castle Cottage) which had been constructed to house the telegraph cable in 1894, and where there was a small postbox. From 1909 this had served as the postmaster's office; there the outgoing mails were packed into the mailbag for despatch, and the incoming letters were sorted for delivery or collection – more often for collection, as Fred Allday, the postmaster from 1898-1926, was known to keep himself up to date by indulging his curiosity about their contents. Both the incoming and outgoing mails had to be carried to or from the beach, for which purpose he was supplied with a donkey – but Irwin the donkey would make himself scarce when he observed that he would be needed.

Fred Allday at the Post Office at the Castle, c.1925

Painting of the Castle by M.F. Heaven dated 1926. The red postbox is visible on the left attached to the telegraph pole. Behind it is the west wall of the Post Office. The postbox was removed in 1927 when the Post Office was closed

The Castle from the south-west in 1922, with Signal Cottages on the left and Coastguard Cottages between them and the Castle. The small structure to the right of the Castle is the flag house

The pair of modern semi-detached houses, facing east, called Signal Cottages, was built for Lloyd's personnel in 1894. Another pair close by, Coastguard Cottages, was built in 1909 and faced south. They may have been suburban in appearance and out of keeping so close to the Castle, but they did at least provide four modern houses, well fitted out and in good habitable condition.

Signal Cottages in the 1920s

Coastguard Cottages in 1951. They were built in 1909. They faced south, and the entrance to the second cottage was at the back. The watchroom at the east end was added in 1925 by the Admiralty as a work place for the watch

The Castle Parade Ground in 1928, with Signal Cottages behind and to the right

The Parade Ground below the magnificent east face of the Castle was occupied by large poles for flags and at the south end was the small square flag house where the signalling apparatus was kept. It was a busy area, dominated by poles, flags and ladders.

MCH was very concerned about the Castle itself, which was in need of repair. The interior held a sad sight – the ruins of the cottages which had been built by W.H. Heaven to house labourers. There were three steps down to a cobbled courtyard, one of which consisted of a half millstone, and a wall to protect the interior from west winds.

The Castle interior in 1950

MCH was anxious that the Castle should be repaired and preserved, so after he became owner of Lundy, he called upon the services of the Society for the Protection of Ancient Buildings whose inspector made a thorough report in 1928 and detailed the work necessary, with a cost estimate of £1,430. The report concludes: 'Although the castle is now in very poor condition and its landward aspect has been somewhat spoiled by the modern buildings nearby, it nevertheless remains impressive and when seen from the landing cove has lost none of its striking grandeur'. In the event, the expense prevented the recommendations in the report from being implemented.

One of the photographs taken in June 1928 which were part of the report on the state of the Castle which was prepared by Mr Charles C. Winmill of the Society for the Protection of Ancient Buildings. The broken-down west wall gives a view of the ruins of the former cottages in the interior. On the right is the signalling flagpole and the small flag house

Tony Langham at the entrance to the former post office, or the Keep, as it was then called. Tony and Myrtle Langham rented it in 1955 for £6 per year, and were thrilled to have a foothold on the island. One holiday was spent there, but it did not afford much comfort. Eventually it was given up as it was needed for islanders

Inside was a porch with a handbasin, but no water; there was a fireplace in the main room, and it was not difficult to gather sticks and wood to light a fire from round the island

Alfred Blackwell: a lover of Lundy

I N AUGUST OF 1925 Mr and Mrs Alfred Blackwell – lovers of Lundy – took the train from Waterloo station, which brought them to Instow station at 8.00pm. After a night at the Marine Hotel, they walked around to Appledore where they boarded the *Lerina*, then limited to twelve passengers. On this occasion the twelve included the Bideford Coroner with his daughter, his clerk, a doctor and a police sergeant who were to conduct an inquest on a visitor who had drowned the previous day. (When Martin Coles Harman bought Lundy, a few months later, he protested against mainland officials landing on the island, but without effect).

The 'Lerina' at anchor in the Landing Bay

Many of the islanders were gathered on the beach and they gave the Blackwells and the other passengers a warm welcome. These included a new blacksmith, and the fisherman, Burke, who came from Ireland, Mrs Barter of the Admiralty Signal Station, Sanders, the store-keeper and postmaster Allday. Miss Sage managed the hotel; her 'wondrous operations resulted in comfort and harmony for all.'

During their stay the Blackwells were treated to a viewing of an amateur film of Lundy life, and then another of 'villainy, heroism and romance.' These had recently been made by Oxford undergraduate friends of the Plunkett-Greene family, who leased the Old Light at that time.

Another diversion was provided by a party of bell-ringers who came for a day and rang for some hours – evidently without hearty appreciation on Blackwell's part, as he adds no comment to the fact. On Sunday Mr Allday, who was also a Lay Reader, conducted services at 11am and 6.30pm.

Alfred Blackwell in 1922 coming through what is now called the 'Monastery Gate' or the 'Blue Door'. Blackwell himself captioned this picture, 'The author at the Garden Entrance to the Manor House'. The gate was originally to give access for islanders to the iron church which was on that part of the island reserved to the Heaven family when they leased the rest of Lundy to the Quarry Company

Blackwell describes a walk to the North End which 'was more purple than two years ago, the heather having grown over the large area which was merely brown. The gold and purple of the middle portion was as luscious as ever (Middle Park). The bracken on the East Side was almost my own height; Mrs B. was invisible when walking through it. Blackberries were there in their customary profusion. We were surprised to learn that as recently as the previous week divers had been working on the wreck [the *Montagu*] bringing up steel plates.'

Congenial visits were made to both lighthouses, and 'the weather was glorious. A peacock strutted in the farmyard garden ...'.

On 4 September the Blackwells tore themselves away: 'My heart was in Lundy's keeping.'

Lundy was sold to Martin Coles Harman a few months after this was written.

Mrs Blackwell outside Barton Cottages in 1922

When he retired from the Metropolitan Police, Mr Blackwell with his wife and their son, Patrick, moved to Instow. He became curator of Barnstaple Athenaeum (Museum) and shore agent for Lundy. He made bookings and sold tickets for the *Lerina*, and – later – for the crossing by air.

Alfred Blackwell's heart was always with Lundy and he was happy to share his stories and memories. When the no-longer-serviceable *Lerina* was sold at auction in 1953, Mr Blackwell bought the board with her name carved on it, which he presented to the island. It is now mounted above the fireplace in the Tavern – a memorial both to its donor and to the island's boat.

In 1945 Alfred Blackwell wrote and published *The Charm and History of Instow (with Lundy Island)*. It was published under the auspices of Instow Parish Council and is now a rare collectors' piece. He also wrote the first informative and documented Lundy bibliography; it was published in the *Transactions of the Devonshire Association*, 1957, Vol. 89 pp.145-152.

> *Going to Lundy with Ruth when I was little meant being collected from the train at Instow and taken to Captain Dark's house at 2 Elm Terrace overnight. We huddled together for warmth in the bed and were woken by Mrs Dark early in the morning for the crossing in the 'Lerina'. Captain Dark would sail in all weathers if he could get to Lundy. I remember menacing seas washing over the deck. To defeat sea-sickness we would eat an apple, or start to sing. It was awful! We both became good sailors later on.*

The *Lerina*

T HE *LERINA* had been bought by Mr Christie to service Lundy, and Martin Coles Harman took over the vessel when he purchased the island. Her skipper was Fred Dark, who served until his death in 1942. Felix Gade, in *My Life on Lundy*, speaks very highly of Captain Dark: 'He was a man who knew the sea, and particularly the sea in the entrance to the Bristol Channel. He was a complete sailorman; I never saw him flustered in the slightest degree, no matter what kind of weather he was experiencing.'

Captain Fred Dark in Lametry Bay in April 1936, with Lundy South Light in the background

The 'Lerina' en route for Lundy, probably in 1922

Mr Gade wrote that the *Lerina* '... was an ideal boat for Lundy in that she could carry a variety of cargoes, and Captain Dark never failed to land passengers, mails, and freight at some point on the island, no matter from what direction the wind blew ... Fred Dark, as master, held only a fishing ticket so, although the *Lerina* was of seventy-two tons gross weight, she could only be licensed to carry twelve passengers. The fare charged was ten shillings return, with half price for children of fourteen and under. She was berthed at Bidna Wharf, Appledore, but passengers and freight were embarked and disembarked from Instow pier because of the railway connection. The *Lerina* was too big to tie up there, so Captain Dark or Jack Branch ferried to and from the vessel, which would be lying fifty to a hundred yards offshore. She was regarded by local seafarers as a very stout and seaworthy craft and I have heard seafaring men in Appledore say that they would rather cross Bideford Bar in rough weather in the *Lerina*, under Captain Dark, than in the R.N.L.I. lifeboat of those days.'

Seen here, arriving at Lundy on the 'Lerina', are (left to right) Jack Branch, the engineer (a challenging task); Captain Fred Dark; the Revd Hugh Muller; Tommy Hornabrook, crew. The occasion was the return of Walter Heaven's ashes to Lundy (see page 66), which is why Revd Muller was aboard and wearing a black arm-band

Then, as now, the normal place to land passengers and cargo was the Landing Beach, but then, as now, easterly winds could make landing difficult, if not impossible. There was, of course, no jetty until 1999. Felix Gade again: 'Captain Dark resorted to a greater variety of landing places than is now commonly used. These included: Pilot's Quay, now not used due to a landslip; Montagu Steps; Smugglers' Path, west of Lametry

Beach, which was difficult both to locate and use; the north-west corner of Lametor, where for many years a length of chain hung from top to bottom, secured to a large steel stake at the top. A landing could be made at a small sand-shingle beach between the south entrance to the Needle's Eye and the Devil's Kitchen; only disclosed on ebb tides, there is easy access to the Devil's Kitchen and from thence, over weedy rocks, to the cove. Apart from the Landing Beach more obvious landing places were the Cove, Hell's Gates and Victoria Beach. Captain Dark also used Ladies' Beach, but the path has since been destroyed by subsidence; Quarry Beach has also suffered subsidence of the path, but was in any case a poor place to beach a boat because of the large stones there; the water at the Miller's Cake is deep enough for a small boat at any tide but the ascent is difficult. Further north, Brazen Ward and Frenchman's Landing are good at all stages of the tide although they have the obvious disadvantage of being far from the village. The ascent at Gannets' Bay is not easy without a rope or ladder, and at the North-East Point there is often broken water.'

Even when the weather was fine, shipping livestock was never easy. These two photographs postdate the *Lerina*, but are a timeless representation of some of the challenges of living on an island.

Right: Hard graft for these five men taking sheep off the island for sale on the mainland in 1957. Tide and wind had to be carefully calculated, and green keep rented until the day of the sale

Below: A tricky problem. The three men on the right are (left to right) Arthur Strick, 'Dave' Davey and John Ogilvie

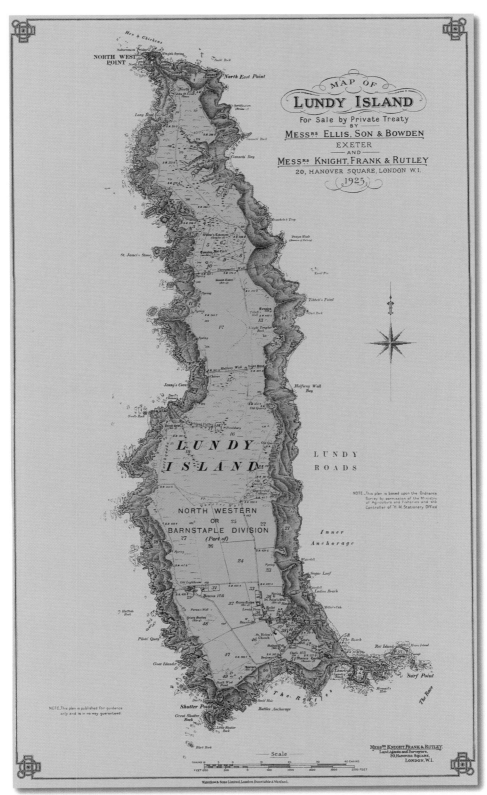

The map of Lundy which appeared in the 1925 catalogue of sale

Lundy is bought

THE PRICE MCH paid for the island was £16,000. The catalogue of sale issued in 1925 describes the Villa, with eight bedrooms, as being available for use as an annexe to the Manor Farm Hotel. That was under the expert management of Miss Nancy Sage.

Exempted from the sale were the Church with its grounds, and the Burial Ground (Beacon Hill), both of which belonged to the Church Commissioners, and the sites of the North and South Lighthouses held by Trinity House. There was not much available accommodation: the Barton cottages were used for staff, and the Old Light was sub-let. Old Light West was disused, as was Stoneycroft, and Fred Allday paid £10 per year rent for the Cliff Bungalow (now Hanmers), but the Quarter Wall Cottages were no longer habitable. In all, the population numbered 31, plus three Trinity House men at each of the north and south lighthouses. Nine of the population were employed for the island, making a weekly wage bill of £13.10s.

Belle Vue Cottages in 1921. The southern property (on the left) was lived in by Fred Allday

The total annual income from tenancies and Rights of Way was £53.10s. In addition, the total of landing fees for the previous year was £126, and MCH took over the GPO mail contract from Christie, at £104 per annum, with the same sum being paid by the Admiralty for the conveyance of personnel and stores.

The farm consisted of 257 acres of cultivated land, mostly pasture, and there was an ample range of farm buildings. Mr Herbert May, a North Devon farmer, had lease of the island until 29 September 1925 at £375 per annum. He did not live on the island, but crossed over regularly, and managed the farm to excellent effect. The fishing was well established, and Lundy waters produced fine lobsters, crabs, and other fish, which were taken across and sold on the mainland. There were herds of 319 sheep, 86 cattle, 99 pigs,

Chris Segens, lobster fisherman, in the 1920s

Lundy lobsters were a gastronomic delicacy of high quality, and more plentiful than they are now. Lobster teas were served in the 'Tea Room' to steamer passengers, price 2/6. Lundy lobsters were also sold on the mainland

110 poultry, with four horses for ploughing and haulage. Also included in the sale were furnishings and fittings, and eight small boats. These, with the *Lerina*, brought the total price to be paid to £25,000. There was also a store at Instow, essential for use with the *Lerina*, that was rented at a cost of £7.10s. per annum.

This photo, c.1926, shows (left-right) Mr Worth (builder), the farm bailiff, Miss Nancy Sage, Miss Phyllis Blackburn, Mr Laws (the agent when MCH bought Lundy), Mr Sullivan, Mrs Vennell

 Albion Harman and Paddy Hanmer once put themselves in the shafts of the donkey cart and went careering about with Rene Gade in the back.

At the age of 40 Martin Coles Harman became the delighted owner of the island. He took over at the end of May's contract, and the formal deeds were completed on 11 November. It was, perhaps, unfortunate that the priest in charge of Lundy, the Revd Muller, vicar of Appledore, was too constant in his attentions for MCH's taste. So, to restrain his enthusiasm, Mr Harman undertook to continue the usual Easter offering of £25, but declared that he would 'deduct £1 for each time he caught Mr Muller on the island.'

Revd Muller being helped to leave Lundy

MCH's objective was not to make a large profit, nor was he ready to carry large losses. What he wanted was for Lundy to remain a remote, wild and primitive island where wildlife predominated, and all lived in peace and seclusion.

Some Lundy residents in 1925. Skipper Benson, who was a regular and welcome visitor, is standing on the left. The back row (left-right) may be Mrs Barber, Violet Coker, ?, Mrs Lang. The musician is unidentified. Mr Lang is sitting, holding the dog, with Miss Coker next to him

Skipper Benson was Danish and huge. In the Tavern there would be dancing to a wind-up gramophone and he and I would dance with me standing on his sea-boots.

Kittiwake Gully, seen from the steps up from the North Light. A similar photograph appeared in 'National Geographic' magazine of May 1947 as part of an article entitled 'Lundy, Treasure Island of Birds'. The piece was written by Col P.T. Etherton who also wrote (with Vernon Barlow) an over-enthusiastic and fanciful book called 'Lundy – The Tempestuous Isle' which was published in 1950. The photo showed kittiwakes and the caption stated that three thousand pairs nested on Lundy in 1939. The bird life of Lundy was one of the aspects of the island about which Martin Coles Harman was most enthusiastic; unlike earlier owners, he saw the birds not as a resource to be exploited but as an asset to be appreciated, conserved and studied

Felix Gade

WHEN MARTIN COLES HARMAN bought Lundy, the then managing agent was Mr Laws, whose home was in Westward Ho! and who was resident on the island as and when necessary. The arrangement was continued *pro tem*, but MCH soon saw the need to have a permanently resident agent on the spot to manage all aspects of island work, and – importantly – one who would share his own philosophy of the island.

He showed perceptive judgement that the right person would have the care of the island at heart, with the ability to exercise a judicious authority and capable of effective oversight of all aspects of island work and its personnel – in other words, a viceroy.

Felix and Rene Gade (and Peggy, the Airedale), photographed probably in the 1920s

In this he proved to be very fortunate. His brother-in-law, Felix Gade, had been an army officer and was awarded the M.C. during the First World War. He and Martin Coles Harman had been friends since childhood, and had shared interests in the countryside and in bird life. He was a tall man, well-built, with a natural authority that was combined with a good sense of humour, and he was a gifted raconteur. He was without experience in estate management, but he understood and shared MCH's wishes and philosophy – not least in upholding Lundy's particular status, over which he was ever strictly watchful.

He arrived on Lundy on 11 November 1926, and on the following day he walked the length and breadth of the island: 'the most wonderful wilderness of land and sea.' He fell completely under the spell of Lundy, with its 'tough, self-reliant, and happy community.' He presided over a population of 31 (excluding the six light keepers) and soon found himself overseer of the farm, the hotel, the boats, and everything else down to the water supply. Yet busy as he was, he was his own secretary, and took great trouble in replying to any letters requesting information. He had a small office opposite the back door of the hotel where, as well as writing the letters, he made up the accounts and dealt with any other paperwork. However, much of his time was spent joining in the work on the farm, or supervising the arrival or departure of the boats, and soon he could turn his hand to every job.

Mr Gade was joined by his wife, Rene, who proved a worthy, popular and hard-working partner. She was a wonderful north-country cook who transformed a stay in the hotel to a gastronomic treat, and she added her own lovely personality to the company.

Felix and Rene Gade, photographed by the late Jack Westcott in 1969. Felix was known as 'Gi' – short for 'Giant' – because of his stature, and Rene was called 'Cheerful' – because she was

> *Mrs Gade sometimes showed the gift of second sight. Once, when a donkey had gone missing, she dreamt that it had fallen between granite boulders on the east side. They went to look, and it was true.*

First things

THERE WERE SOME PROBLEMS. Feral cats abounded, and five shillings (25p) was offered to the workforce for every dead cat brought in, which was a welcome addition to wages (ten shillings a week at that time). This was very effective in clearing the island of cats, with the result that the number of rats, both brown and black, being prolific breeders, increased to the point where MCH was forced to call in pest exterminators. But it was impossible to clear them completely, and the exterminators were called in for a second onslaught. Elimination was seemingly impossible, but the islanders were encouraged to continue the slaughter, using ferrets, with the reward of a certificate of proficiency in rat killing.

No 50

Lundy Rat Killers

CERTIFICATE OF PROFICIENCY

I hereby certify that

is a skilled and tireless rat killer

Marisco Castle Lundy. 19

A Certificate of Proficiency in rat killing, with a typically elegant vignette by John Dyke. Rats were eliminated from Lundy only in 2006 under the Seabird Recovery Programme

Rabbits were also present in super-abundance to the detriment of the pasture, although many were in very poor condition. Trapping, even of thousands, was effective only to a limited extent. Despite this, it is surprising that MCH brought in some Angora and Chinchilla rabbits to improve the stock. At that time there was no question of farming the rabbits – either for food or for fur – as the trapping and transport costs would exceed any profits.

Bob Helson and friend – champion rabbit-catchers

Lighting was by oil lamps and candles. Transport was by horse and cart, for which there were two carts – the haulage of goods both incoming and outgoing must have been slow and heavy work, and difficult across the stony beach. The mailbag would be landed first, and taken up, then the cargo was sorted into perishables and passengers' luggage. The remainder was stored in the black shed alongside the fishermen's cottage until it could be taken to the top – inevitably a slow process.

When the boat comes in ... The 'Lerina' anchored in the Landing Bay, the transport waiting

At first the sheep shearing was carried out by the use of hand clippers (some 250 head). There were some farm machines, and a paraffin 4½ h.p. engine in the barn, used for a threshing box, chaff cutter, grist mill, circular saw and – later – a shearing machine, although for that it was not really sufficiently powerful.

The work was hard; the men would be engaged on the farm, as well as working on the beach to load and unload cargoes, including livestock, and would take on running repairs. The women worked in the hotel and the laundry and, sometimes, in the gardens. There was no school for the children; doctors came on call from the mainland when needed, which would take several hours, and the vicar came across to hold services at intervals.

Mr Gade underwent an enforced and quite sharp period of learning in managing and caring for the livestock – and subsequently the ponies – but he was alert, intelligent, and committed to succeed, and able to take the workforce along with him. To begin with, Mr May was a source of advice and help, although MCH's dictum to try to carry the island on its own resources, without cash subsidies, was not possible. Lundy was exposed to strong winds, depended on the catchment of rainwater, and every item that was brought to the island or taken ashore had to bear the cost of transport.

 I remember rat-killing in the Farm. The party would go at night to the Grain Store, next to the Slaughterhouse, with dogs and ferrets. The bins were rattled and beaten with sticks and the dogs barked – the noise was incredible!

Embellishing the island

ARTIN COLES HARMAN wanted to furnish his island with a variety of wildlife – both for his own enjoyment, and to interest the visitors on whom the island depended for a good part of its income. The North End was overgrown, and it was hoped that some animals might help to remedy that, while others could add variety to the island scene. There was plenty of pasture, but he was perhaps over-optimistic in the numbers that could be sustained. It may be said that his enthusiasm was greater than his expertise, but the long-term results have been positive.

The first move was to add to the range of geese, although it proved to be the case that they needed supplementary feeding, which was altogether too expensive. Next, the number of goats was increased to 25, as it was hoped that they might keep down the then-extensive brambles; they were allowed free range, and their number increased rapidly, so that it was necessary to cull them from time to time. An effort was made to milk them, but it proved to be impossible as they were too wild. However, they were undoubtedly picturesque poised on the northwestern rocks.

Goats at the North End, still doing their job of being picturesque

Hares were not successful, and partridges and red squirrels did not survive for very long, but the Golden Orfe thrived in the quarry pond, and later some were moved to the Rocket Pole pond, which they share amiably with the mallard ducks later introduced by Albion Harman. MCH was presented with two rock wallabies, which unfortunately drowned themselves as they were not used to water, and two swans placed on Pondsbury flew away since their wings had not been clipped.

Construction of a fence across the island at Quarter Wall was started preparatory to the introduction of deer, but the work presented difficulties and was not completed before 32 head of Fallow deer and eight head of Sika deer were brought to the island early in 1927. Landing them in the dinghies was very difficult indeed, and not a task in which the Lundy workforce or the boat's crew had any experience. Mr Gade later wrote that the day was 'one of the most arduous of many arduous days on Lundy,' and that the deer gravitated to the shrubbery and the rhododendron thickets around Millcombe to the detriment of farm crops. A year later, in his enthusiasm, MCH sent a further fifteen red deer that were even more troublesome to land than the first shipment; the men were working against time and tide and the inclination of the deer to go for a swim. Three of the deer died, and of a batch of eight deer calves sent to strengthen the herd, five died due to intolerance of cow's milk. However, deer were – and the remaining Sika deer still are – a very popular attraction for visitors.

New Forest ponies joined the variety of animals in 1928. They have done well and are now a distinct breed. They have been cared for by members of staff, assisted by knowledgeable regular visitors, and have been sought as good-natured riding ponies. They have also shown well in national gymkhanas. In 1944, Soay sheep were brought to Lundy and have thrived ever since, making a contribution to the landscape, to conservation management and to the Tavern menu.

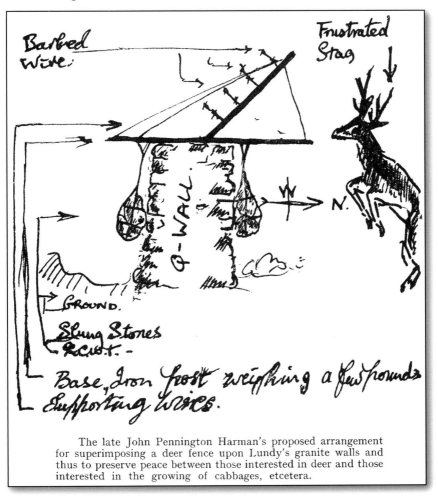

The late John Pennington Harman's proposed arrangement for superimposing a deer fence upon Lundy's granite walls and thus to preserve peace between those interested in deer and those interested in the growing of cabbages, etcetera.

In 1947, MCH arranged for a modern reprint of 'Some Account of the Island of Lundy' by George Steinman Steinman, originally published in 1837, which had become a rarity. As a tribute to his late son (see page 94) he included John P. Harman's sketch of his idea for a fence which would keep the deer north of the Quarter Wall without damaging the wall itself. (The frontispiece photograph is from that reprint)

Lundy lights

THERE WERE FOUR KEEPERS for each of the lighthouses, and at any time one keeper would be on shore leave. They often helped with various tasks on the island on their free days, and joined the company in the tavern, an integral part of life on Lundy. (Trinity House classified lighthouses as 'shore stations' – such as Hartland Point, where supplies arrive by land – or 'rock stations' – for example, Bishop Rock, where supplies and relief could be problematic. Lundy was supplied by sea and was a 'rock station' – but a rock station where off-duty keepers could visit a pub).

The keepers were very hospitable when people made the journey (down) to the North Light or (up) to the South Light. Visitors would receive mugs of strong tea, and a spoon to help themselves from the tin of condensed milk and to the biscuits. The hosts were always pleased to receive newspapers or magazines, and enjoyed meeting a wide variety of visitors. On their first visit they would be conducted to admire the light installations, where the brass gleamed brilliantly, and everything was immaculate. At the North Light the lantern was bedded in a bath of mercury, which gave it a particular interest.

The North Light when it was fully manned. The Trinity House flag is flying (upwards, in a strong wind!) from the flagpole. In the foreground are the steps leading down to the landing stage in a gully. In the bottom right of the picture, a cable is just visible against the background of the sea. This brought up supplies – see the photo on the next page

Supplies for the North Light were transferred by cable from the Trinity House ship at anchor off the N.W. end to a grassy platform that led across to the lighthouse. The distance was not inconsiderable, and the goods heavy, so a small railway was installed that was used by the lightkeepers to move the ingoing or outgoing cargoes to the point where the cable connection to the ship was installed. Joy rides were strictly forbidden!

Crew at the South Light unloading stores from the cable which led up to the lighthouse from its anchor on the sea bed (see also the photo on page 15)

Principal Keeper Harold Hall, who served at both Lundy North and Lundy South, in the 1930s

Lundy North was automated in 1991 and Lundy South in 1994 and the lights are now monitored and controlled from Harwich. The removal of the Trinity House keepers ended a long and happy relationship between the lighthouses and the islanders. It is beyond question that the lighthouses fulfilled vital functions in warning ships of Lundy's rocky coast, although the explosives detonated at the South Light in foggy weather, later succeeded by the hooting of the foghorn, which sometimes continued all night, was undoubtedly not quite so well appreciated by would-be sleepers. The North Light lost its foghorn some years ago, and the fog signal of the South Light was finally switched off in July 2012.

 When we visited 'Daddy' Hall at the North Light, we would take the keepers fresh milk. They used to bake their own bread.

Lundy calling ...

WHILE UPHOLDING proper respect for the Crown, MCH regarded Lundy as having a similar position to other overseas members of the Empire, and he described it as being a 'vest-pocket dominion.' By this he meant that it was independent in its own administration, while remaining absolutely loyal in matters that were of national concern.

With this in mind he wrote to his solicitor when he bought the island to request him to write to the Chancellor of the Exchequer to state that the island was ready to pay its proper share against the burden of the costs of the war (1914-18). This was to be an affirmation of Lundy's loyalty, and was compared to Jersey. At the same time he was very much against the idea of mainland authorities ever having any place or personnel on the island.

After the GPO mail contract was ended, and the telegraph cable was broken, MCH closed down the coastguard station in 1928. There was sadness when the coastguard station was closed – the personnel were sorry to leave, and the islanders were very sorry to see them go, as they had been a welcome addition to life on the island – and there were protests from ship owners and the Board of Trade. This was due to concern that there was then no rapid means of communication if a ship were in distress or there was a wreck. An agreement was reached that the island would be responsible for the life-saving apparatus, and the cable would be replaced by a radio-telephone. Permission was given for Mr Gade to be the telephone operator, although he was not obliged to take the complicated examination that was usually required.

Practice firing of the rocket life-saving apparatus

Above: Felix Gade speaking to Hartland on the radio. This photo was taken after the radio had been moved from the Old Light to the Radio Room in the Hotel yard (below)

Mr Gade became Lloyd's agent on Lundy and undertook the responsibility of reporting to Lloyds of London when any vessel sheltered off Lundy and when it resumed its passage, or if any vessel was in difficulty. This would be via corresponding radio telephone equipment at Hartland Point Coastguard station which would transmit messages both to and from Lundy and Trinity House.

It was a tremendous advantage to the island to have such direct communication. Regular calls were made daily at 9.00am and 4.00pm – to which the whole of North Devon would tune in, so that nothing remained private – but it was very efficient and friendly, and very warm relationships were maintained between the two stations. Mr Gade would radio Hartland twice every day – 'Lundy calling, Lundy calling' – both to receive and send messages. Attentive watch was kept on shipping around the island, and the lighthouse keepers were vigilant. The radio telephone was initially set up at the Old Light, which was thought to offer the best reception, and all went very well indeed.

Family holidays: early years

MARTIN COLES HARMAN went to Lundy for Christmas in 1926, taking with him his two sons – John, then 12 years old, and Albion, 10 years – and a few friends. Because of a strong easterly wind they had to land on rocks on the West Side at night; a real baptism of fire, as the landing was at Montagu Steps. The

Montagu Steps in rough weather. Landing was sometimes made here when easterly winds persisted and it was a testing experience. Diana Keast remembers a challenging occasion when she had to carry up a 14lb ham

Colum Ansell, the family chauffeur, with John and Albion near Tibbets in 1925

passengers had to climb the steep and rough path to the top, and all the luggage and Christmas provisions had to be carried up, one by one, by three of the island men, and then taken by cart across to the hotel. When the party returned to view the site of their landing the next morning they were horror-struck, but quite proud of themselves. Captain Dark of the *Lerina* described it as 'a coarse passage.'

In his happy enthusiasm to share the pleasures of his island, and his optimism, a pheasant shoot was arranged for Christmas Day, but unhappily that also ran into trouble. The pheasant poults he had imported had prospered, and the shoot took place along the east sideland, but that was heavily covered by gorse, deep bracken, and brambles. It proved impossible for dogs to retrieve the fallen birds, and this disappointment caused MCH to burn off the cover, but unfortunately he had not reckoned on an east wind which carried the fire along the side land as far as the Quarter Wall. Mercifully the rain fell the next day, and the lost rhododendrons were replaced by larch saplings, but these – unhappily – were consumed by the rabbits and goats. It is sad to think of such happy enthusiasms meeting these frustrations, but Lundy can be unyielding to impulses, however enthusiastic.

Sharing his new enthusiasm with the family. Above: MCH's parents visiting Lundy in the late 1920s.

Right: Martin and Amy Harman visiting the North Light at Easter 1926

Beyond that, Felix Gade did record that the hardest task he ever had to carry out on Lundy was to push MCH's elderly Aunt Elizabeth in her Bath chair from the beach to the hotel, although it is also recorded that she was able to ride one of the horses to the North End. As he was writing in the 1970s, the memory was evidently deeply engrained.

On the Landing Beach in the 1920s. The two adults on the left are family friends. On the right is Martin Coles Harman surrounded by his children, left to right: John, Albion, Diana, Ruth. On the right is Miss James – 'Jamie' – the children's governess

Mrs Harman feeding the lambs in 1926 or 1927

From Farmhouse to Hotel

MARTIN COLES HARMAN hoped that his friends, and others who shared his interest and enjoyment of Lundy, would like to come and stay on the island, and while not envisaging any smart hotel, he did wish to offer moderate comfort and convenience. Consequently he set about making alterations and repairs, which united the various sections of the farmhouse building into an integral whole. The space between the original north wing and the farmhouse was made into a games room with a billiard table (now the floor of Castle Cottage) and thus presented a complete east frontage to the hotel. Another priority was to add conveniences and another bathroom – he having declared the intention of having as many bathrooms on the island as there were bells for the church. After the works, the hotel re-opened in March 1927.

THE MANOR FARM HOTEL, LUNDY

Above: Manor Farm Hotel with a unified east façade. Compare this with the view on page 18

Right: a detail of the northern end of the east frontage in 1922, before the work to raise the roof height to a uniform level

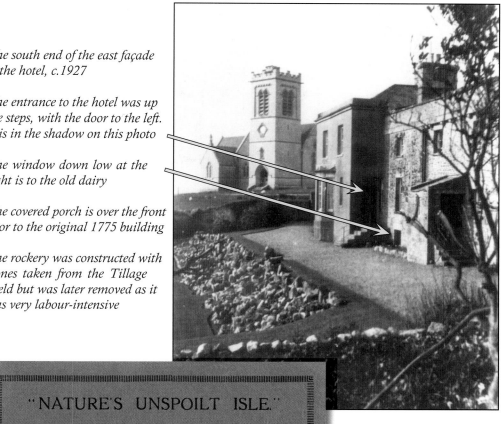

The south end of the east façade of the hotel, c.1927

The entrance to the hotel was up the steps, with the door to the left. It is in the shadow on this photo

The window down low at the right is to the old dairy

The covered porch is over the front door to the original 1775 building

The rockery was constructed with stones taken from the Tillage Field but was later removed as it was very labour-intensive

"NATURE'S UNSPOILT ISLE."

LUNDY

INFORMATION
COMMUNIC
ACCOMMO

This small (5½×4⅛ inches) brochure (above) was produced c.1928 and includes the tariff for the Manor Farm Hotel (right)

Manor Farm Hotel, LUNDY,
NORTH DEVON.

Tariff en Pension.

Apartments and Board, including attendance—
JULY 1st to SEPT. 30th . . £4 4 0 to £5 5 0 per week.
Other months . . . . £3 3 0 to £4 4 0 per week.
Morning Tea 9d.
Reduced Terms for Families and Parties and Long Periods.

Bedrooms	5/- to 7/6 per night.
Breakfast 9 a.m.	2/-
Luncheon, 1 o'clock	2/6
Afternoon Tea, served in Lounge, 4 to 4.30 p.m. .	1/6
Dinner, 7.30 p.m.	3/6

Telegrams : "SAGE, LUNDY-ISLAND-COASTGUARD-STATION."
(ONE WORD).

These two photographs, taken in 1960, show the back (west) side of the hotel that bordered the road.

This is the north yard and shows, at top left, the window of the bathroom that was added

Below it was 'the bogey hole'. The hot water boiler was there, and consequently in wet weather it was generously draped with dripping garments, optimistically squashed in there to dry by their owners. It became impossible to shut the door

On the left were coal and wood stores

This photograph shows the back entrance to the hotel where there was a W.C. The kitchen and scullery were on the right

The block on the left was a Heaven addition of a dairy and a meat room. MCH built staff bedrooms above it. Diana Keast remembers that Arthur Strick in the 1960s called these rooms 'Bloody Pentonville'!

These plans of the hotel were drawn in 1973 by Colin Taylor and Myrtle Langham (Ternstrom). They are not scaled drawings. North is to the right.

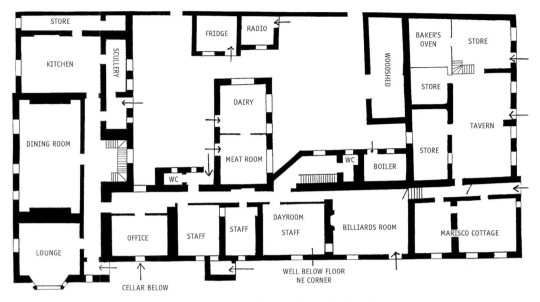

Above: the ground floor. Below: the first floor

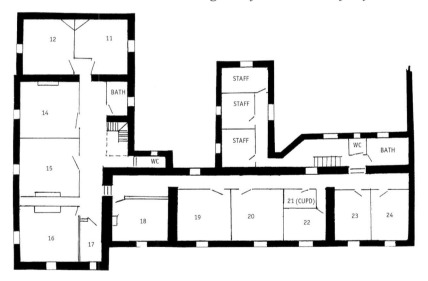

On the north (right) of the ground floor plan is the entrance to the Tavern. This is still the entrance to the Marisco Tavern, which has been extended to the east to take in Marisco Cottage. The store on the top right is now Reception and the Office. The south wing (Lounge and Dining Room) have been demolished and the Kitchen rebuilt as Square Cottage. The Fridge and Radio rooms have been amalgamated into the modern Radio Room. The Dairy and Meat Rooms have been removed to create a grassed square, and the main run of rooms on the east side, from Office to Dayroom Staff have been rebuilt as Old House South and Old House North.

Some of the interiors are shown in these snapshots which were taken in the 1970s, before the Hotel building was closed and totally remodelled by the Landmark Trust.

The south-east corner of the Lounge, where afternoon tea was served. The table was excellent for games of cards, or even not-very-serious séances. The large window looked east over the Hotel garden. This window is now in the Tavern

Above left: the south-west corner of the Lounge

Above right: the Billiards Room

Right: One of the smaller double rooms, Room 23 was above the Billiards Room. The window overlooked the hotel garden. The jug and basin were for one's morning and evening washes. Hot water was brought in cans and the big jug held cold water

The Dining Room. There is a hatch through to the Kitchen

Above: The entrance to the hotel from the back door in the south courtyard, and Mr Gade's office – always a busy place. Hanging from the coat hook is the Spring 1971 edition of the 'Illustrated Lundy News'

To the right the corridor led to the south wing: Kitchen, Lounge, Dining Room and the stairs (right), which made a gracious curve. At the bottom of the stairs on the left was the passage to the Billiard Room and the Bar

Lundy links

A BRIGHT IDEA to extend Lundy's attractions did not stem from MCH, but he did not object when a plan which had been initiated by his previous agent, Laws, with some enthusiasts from South Wales, came to fruition.

A nine-hole golf course was laid out on Aclands Moor, designed by Major Sullivan of Southerndown Golf Club, near Bridgend. There was a grand opening day on 31 July 1927 with about 100 guests, when Mrs Harman performed the opening ceremony and drove off the first ball. The course had a total length of 2,630 yards, and was on 'a breezy position on a stretch of moorland for which par was 36.' The hope was that it would prove an attraction and bring more visitors to the island. The first match was played between two Welsh teams, one professional and one amateur. The amateurs won, and it was politely said that it was 'an interesting course', although further work was needed to bring it up to scratch. All the party were served with Lundy lobster lunches, and a cup was presented for an annual competition between the islanders.

A lean-to for the equipment was built against the wall of Old Light West that was also intended to be a club-house, but the golf course was not good enough – nor the weather reliable enough – to bring numbers of golfers to the island, and it was running at a loss, so the venture was closed in 1928. Diana Keast recounts that in 1952 it was her idea for the disused competition cup to become Inez Harman's christening mug.

On the new golf course in 1927, and dressed for the occasion. Left to right: Florence Cole (eldest sister of MCH), Miss Rosie Entwistle, Mrs Amy Harman, Felix Gade

On the steps from the Hotel to the tennis lawn, ready for the lobster lunch. Amy Harman is in the centre of the front row. The girl on her left is her goddaughter, the daughter of Parkin, the gardener

Closed, but not abandoned, since in 1980 a young visitor, Patrick Penny, founded the 'Lundy Ancient and Necropolistic Golf Club' to arrange for five-yearly matches of no serious character, though these have now lapsed.

However the course can still be identified, and occasionally the stouthearted will take a club or two for a round. The Lundy Field Society, during its members' week visit in June 2000, enjoyed a memorable game when the fog made the visibility half the length of each hole.

Laughter on the links in June 2000

Local Rules

1. The ball must hit the stone or the flag to hole out.

2. Rabbit holes - drop within two club lengths (not nearer the flag) without penalty.

3. Anyone hitting a grockle is awarded an automatic par for this hole.

4. An award will be presented to the player with the highest number of 'puffins' (25 strokes over par).

5. Anyone who scores a hole in one buys a round for all the competitors and plays the rest of the course blindfolded.

6. All cow pats to be played out of.

7. Bracken may only be cut with disseting scissors.

8. Snooker shots are only allowed on the greens.

10. Only the golf ball of an immediate opponent may be trampled into the ground.

11. Ricocheting off your partner is not allowed.

12. Drunkenness and irresponsibility is encouraged - anyone Not caught drinking on the golf course will be disqualified.

13. The sea is casual water and need not be played out of.

Score ... Card

Lundy Ancient and Necropolistic Golf Club: An Introduction to Lundy.

The Old Course Ackland's Moor

The 1990 Lundy A&NGC Open Golf Championship

Hole	PAR	YARDS	MARKER	OPPONENT
1	4	267	---------	---------
2	4	305	---------	---------
3	4	356	---------	---------
4	4	300	---------	---------
5	3	100	---------	---------
6	5	405	---------	---------
7	3	170	---------	---------
8	5	410	---------	---------
9	4	317	---------	---------

The Lundy A&N Golf Club   Founded 1980

The club seeks to promote the study and playing of the most noble of sports, among the native population and visitors to the Island. The open competition is held on the old course every five years whilst friendly games are held on all the courses on an irregular and informal basis. The AGM is held whenever and wherever a quorum of members gather in convivial surroundings within the confines of the western hemisphere. Modest grants for members of the committee are requested to assist with their bar bills. Details of membership can be obtained with great difficulty from any committee member while in the vicinity of the Marisco Tavern, any alcohol purchased for committee members can be redeemed as green fees.

A less than serious approach to golf on Lundy

1. Cesspit Drive

Tee near old light with Ladies tee 50 ft north. Green: the arrow banks of the green are curved westerly and are obvious with stones on top. They are a little east of a stream.

2. The Devil's Burn

Tee 75 ft south west of arrow banks; 10 ft west of a path. Green: about 40 yards east south east of telegraph pole 30.

3. Biggles Ditch

Tee about 40 yards almost due east of telegraph pole 30. Green: about 75 yards south of high pond on edge of bracken.

4, Cole's Revenge

Tee 25 yards south east of third green. Green: slightly raised circular, 20 yards to south east.

5. Quarter Wall Quagmire

Tee about 20 yards north of fourth green, by quarter wall. Green: 90 yards due east.

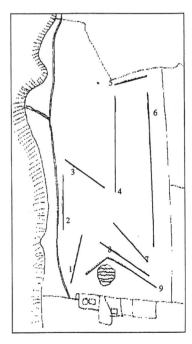

6. Who's got the hip flask?

Tee in line between fifth green and old light, about 40/50 yards from the fifth green. Green: between wall and seventh tee.

7. Penny's Pat

Tee approximately 50 yards north of rubble, near a wall running north. Green:near aircraft ditch.

8. The Bees Tee

Tee 75 yards north east of arrow banks Green 75 yards north of 9th tee.

9. Langham's Last

Tee 75 yards north of lighthouse field wall, 10 yards west of north running wall. Green: raised near old hut at Old Light.

19. What's Yours?

Tee: No thanks I must buy the committee a beer each. Green: Only in the morning.

Two brides

M ARTIN COLES HARMAN became an accomplished escort for Lundy brides. When one of his secretaries, Miss Mary Nell, was to be married in 1928 he very gladly, and generously, arranged for her wedding to take place on Lundy. Twenty guests were carried over by the *Lerina* and accommodated in the hotel; the necessary white ribbons and the music for the wedding march were sent for, and MCH gave the bride away in style. The reception took place in the hotel dining room, and the newly married Mr and Mrs Considine then spent their honeymoon on the island. The celebrant was the Revd Muller who married them by licence.

Lundy wedding fashions in 1928 (right) and 1954 (below). The underdressed horse is John Vicary's 'Gay Boy', and probably wasn't on the guest list

Miss Eva Zoref had no family in England, and MCH gave her away when in 1954 she married Don Mayes, one of the Lundy pilots. A very happy reception was held in the hotel, with all the islanders and the bridegroom's family among the guests. Eva was very lively, warm-hearted and popular; she rented Brambles bungalow, and spent as much of her time on Lundy as her nursing profession would allow. She was expert on her guitar, and would sing a range of sometimes off-beat, amusing, and much appreciated songs, with which she would happily entertain the company in the bar. The hot favourite concerned 'a medicinal compound ... efficacious in every case.' Don and Eva settled in Cheltenham and raised their family there.

The *Maria Kyriakides*

O N THE MORNING of Monday 25 March 1929 the keepers at the South Light informed Mr Gade that there was a ship ashore on the rocks on the East Side, so a search party set off and found it in the area of the quarries. It was a Greek cargo ship, the *Maria Kyriakides*. Some of the crew had gone off in their lifeboat towards the landing beach, but it was unfortunately during the period when the telegraph cable was broken, so no message could be sent to report on the wreck before the *Lerina* arrived on the following Friday.

At their own request, although their quarters aboard would have been habitable, the crew were accommodated on shore – the officers in the hotel and the others in Bramble Villa. They were a rather a rough lot, and only the captain was able to speak English. Mr Gade was Lloyd's sub-agent and responsible for the ship and its contents until the agent and surveyor should attend, and when they duly arrived the ship was declared to be a wreck and the crew were taken ashore. The captain's chair was landed on the island and is still there. The most useful of the wreck bounty were some bags of coal, which were shared equally between the island householders.

Although seriously holed, she was successfully refloated the next year and towed to Ilfracombe. However, the damage was deemed to be not worth repair, so she was later towed to Newport and broken up.

The 'Maria Kyriakides' aground near the quarries
Inset: the ship's bell, which is now in Millcombe House

Postage and puffins

MARTIN COLES HARMAN took over the Royal Mail contract from A.L. Christie, whereby the mails were carried weekly between Instow and Lundy, per the *Lerina*, for £208 per annum. But when the contract was due for renewal Harman did not comply. He wished to negotiate a new agreement whereby he would issue Lundy stamps to cover the cost of transport to and from the mainland, and the onward delivery, so that the GPO would then forward outgoing mails as usual.

This was not acceptable to the authorities, and so MCH – to use his own words – 'dismissed the Post Office' at the end of 1927. Capt. Dark continued to carry the mails to and from the Sub Post Office at Instow, for which MCH provided two mail bags, with locks, to which the island postmaster also had keys. Mr Gade took over responsibility for distributing the in-mails, and despatching the out-mails, and he also held a stock of GPO stamps. He worked from his office at the hotel, so there was no longer a Lundy Post Office.

From 1 January 1928 to 31 October 1929 the mails were transported free of charge, including those for the lighthouses. MCH regarded the loss of the GPO payments for the contract and the rent of the post office as very minor, because he relished the satisfaction of Lundy's seeing off a government authority.

"THIS SCEPTRED ISLE."

[In the course of an appeal in the King's Bench Division, Mr. HARMAN, the "king" of Lundy, stated that the island had its own stamps and postal service, adding, "I dismissed the G.P.O."]

KINGS once were kings: when NERO fired
  Old Rome and watched destruction dealt,
Men thought him mad or ill-inspired,
  But still he made his presence felt.

In later days our HENRY too,
  In pride of power and native force,
Brushed from his path a CLEMENT who
  Held different views upon divorce.

No king, but kingly, CROMWELL spake
  In accents of command; he bent
His eye upon the mace; said, "Take
  Away this bauble!"—and it went.

We hardly hoped that we could meet
  Such men; and yet can History show
A speech more royal, more complete
  Than "I dismissed the G.P.O."?

'Punch', 21 January 1931

The first 1 puffin stamp from 1929. This one bears a 1931 postmark

But the idea of a Lundy stamp remained, both as off-setting mail costs and raising revenue. Accordingly, in 1929 he commissioned Messrs Bradbury Wilkinson to design two stamps. They were to be designated in puffins instead of pence, the 1 puffin stamp in blue, and the half puffin in pink. Both outgoing and incoming mail carried these stamps on the address side and the recipients were charged the appropriate 'puffinage'.

At first the Lundy stamps were put next to the British stamps, but objections were raised by the GPO as this was against regulations, and so the Lundy stamps were put on the backs of the envelopes.

The stamps aroused a good deal of interest, have proved to be very popular, and since then many designs and values have been produced that have served the island postal office. They bring revenue, and the various issues reflect aspects of the island and its history. Between 1929 and 1969, when Lundy was sold to the National Trust, there were another 29 varied issues or overprints, many of which are now very rare, and eagerly sought after by collectors. Many collectors are also visitors to Lundy.

Commemorative stamp issued in 1969 to mark the fortieth anniversary of the Lundy postal service. The drawing by John Dyke shows Fred Allday who was the GPO postmaster in the early twentieth century and the donkey he used to carry the mails

How immensely delighted MCH would have been to see the success of the stamps, the many various issues, and to know that a collection of Lundy stamps is held in the British Library Philatelic Collections. Puffin stamps are in everyday use, and the collectors have formed their own small, but flourishing, club. The Lundy postal system is the oldest operational private postal service in the world.

Postcard showing a selection of Lundy stamps from the first sixty years

> The mail bag was always last down and first up from the beach, frequently humped along by Ruth, me, or any willing Hanmers, boyfriends etc. It was heavy canvas, and secured with a brass padlock.

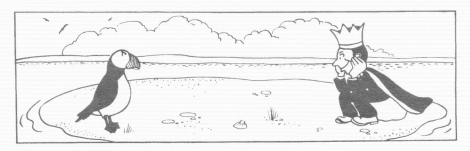

THE STAMPS OF LUNDY ISLAND
— and the Strange Story of the Man who Thought he was King of Puffinland

These stamps tell an extraordinary tale — about a man who set himself up as king of an island off the coast of England only a few years ago.

The story begins in 1925, when a wealthy Englishman, Martin Harman, purchased the tiny 3-mile-long island of Lundy off the coast of Devon. Presently Mr. Harman had an idea. "Since I am the owner of this island", he mused, "why shouldn't I also be king?" The idea seemed to make sense to Mr. Harman, and like an intelligent ruler, he proceeded to coin money and issue postage stamps for use by the island's inhabitants. The stamps and coins bore a picture of the puffin, a paunchy bird with a supercilious expression which inhabits the island in great numbers.

At first all went well with the Liliputian kingdom. But in 1931 the British government got wind of what was going on. By Jove! Chap coining money, don't you know. Bear looking into, and all that, eh what? The result was that "King" Harman was summoned to court, and charged with unlawfully coining money. A justice of the King's Bench fixed a stern eye on the monarch of Lundy.

"*Who* did you say is sovereign of Lundy?" asked the judge.

"I am!" stated Mr. Harman emphatically. "And as sovereign of Lundy I coined puffins and half-puffins as I have a right to do".

But the court took a dim view of His Majesty King Harman's regal pretensions. King Harman suddenly found that he was an ex-king, was fined 5 pounds, and was ordered to relinquish his royal prerogatives.

Today, Lundy is part of the British Empire, and former King Harman is an ordinary subject of King George. But the stamps remain, a fascinating item for collectors, unique in postal history. For they are the only British stamps ever issued — not by the British government, not by a British dominion, commonwealth, colony or possession — but by a now private citizen, His Exalted Ex-Royal Highness, King Harman I, Ex-Monarch of Puffinland!

LITTLETON STAMP CO., Littleton, N. H.

Information/advertising sheet published by the Littleton Stamp Company of Littleton, New Hampshire, U.S.A., probably in the late 1940s

Pennies and puffins

PERHAPS INSPIRED by the stamps marking Lundy as being separate from the mainland, MCH then decided to mint Lundy copper coins. The contract was placed with the Birmingham Mint (Ralph Heaton & Sons) for two copper coins in denominations equivalent to the penny and the halfpenny. The obverse of the larger coin showed a profile head of MCH in relief, with the wording around it, 'Martin Coles Harman, 1929'. The reverse showed the relief figure of a puffin, in profile, with the inscription around it of 'Lundy One Puffin.' The obverse of the smaller coin shows a relief profile of a puffin head, with 'Lundy' written above, and 'Half Puffin' below. Instead of a milled edges, each coin carried the inscription, 'Lundy Lights and Leads'.

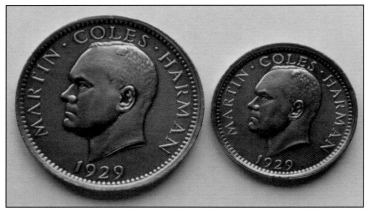

Above: the obverse of the two coins, showing MCH's head where the head of the sovereign would be on a normal penny. Below: the reverse of the Puffin and Half Puffin

From 15 November 1929 all pence and halfpence in use on the island were replaced by the Harman coins. This meant that some coins would inevitably find their way back to the mainland, as indeed happened. And the authorities took notice. All was well until the Chief Constable of Devon came to Lundy to ask for an interview with Mr Gade, who introduced himself as the Chief Constable of Lundy, and confirmed that the Harman coins were in use on Lundy.

As a result of this visit MCH was summoned to appear before the Court at Bideford on 15 April 1930 to answer for breach of the law that restricts the minting and issue of coins to the Crown. He refused to plead as he considered Lundy to be out of the Court's jurisdiction, but this argument was not accepted, and although the case was conducted in good spirit, he was found guilty and fined £5 with 15 guineas costs, which he paid under protest. He felt that this was a modest cost for the opportunity to promote Lundy's status, although it meant that the coins had to be removed from circulation on the island.

MCH appealed against the court's having jurisdiction over Lundy, and conducted his own case before the Lord Chief Justice with aplomb and good humour. Although the Lord Chief Justice congratulated MCH on the conduct of his case, the appeal was dismissed. So from then on the coins were sold as souvenirs at face value.

The important issue arising from the coin case was that it provided an authoritative definition of Lundy's legal status, that was given by the Lord Chief Justice: 'Lundy constitutes part of His Majesty's Dominion … and there is no doubt that the English Common law … applies on the Island.'

The coins remained on sale for some years at increasing prices. In 1965 Albion Harman had sets of replica coins made from the original dies by Pinches Ltd as presentation items. In this case they are not inscribed round the edge and have the year 1965 instead of 1929. The originals continue to increase in value as collectors' pieces and sell typically for £10-£20 on eBay.

MCH WAS KEEN TO PUBLICISE Lundy, not blatantly, but with various devices. From the lighthouses he developed his motto that *Lundy Lights and Leads*. This was printed in green on two-and-a-half inch wide white adhesive tape that was used for many years for packets and parcels.

The damp atmosphere of Lundy did not lend itself to keeping in good condition packets of cigarettes that were to be sold in the bar. To remedy this MCH arranged for special packaging in tins, which – naturally – carried the motto, *Lundy Lights & Leads*.

Heavens and Harmans

THE HEAVEN FAMILY of Bristol owned Lundy from 1834 until 1917, when it was purchased by A.L. Christie, from whom Martin Coles Harman bought the island. Walter Heaven, the last of that family to own Lundy, had emigrated to Australia, where he died, in Beechworth, Victoria, in 1929. In 1930 his sister, Mrs Marion Heaven of Bristol, arranged with MCH for his ashes to be brought to Lundy. The ashes were buried within the grave of his grandfather, William Hudson Heaven, at the Beacon Hill cemetery, and a plaque was placed behind the base of the monumental cross.

The bier with urn and wreaths about to be loaded on to the 'Lerina' at Appledore.
© R.L. Knight Ltd, Barnstaple

Marion Heaven had married a cousin and thus retained the family name. She was born in Australia but grew up on Lundy, and each year the family spent their holidays on the island with their relations. She and her husband continued to visit the island and were well known to Felix Gade.

Their daughter, Eileen Heaven, continued to come to Lundy from her home in Portishead to spend a week on the island each year. Whatever the weather or the temperature, she would have a swim in the sea. She was of a sweet nature, and never presumed on her family name.

Eileen Heaven above Millcombe in 1965

The *Taxiarchis*

THE WRECK of the Greek ship *Taxiarchis* on 28 March 1931 was a major event, when the entire personnel of Lundy, led by Felix Gade, showed extraordinary tenacity and fortitude.

The ship went aground in Halfway Wall Bay, very close to where the *Maria Kyriakides* had come to grief two years earlier. The master was reluctant to authorise the abandonment of the ship, despite the appalling weather conditions, and the only person on board who spoke good English was the radio operator – a Welshman employed by the Marconi company. Communication between the ship and the Lundy team who were standing by with the rocket life-saving apparatus was non-existent for much of the time. The Clovelly and Appledore lifeboats attended, but their attempts to contact the ship were ignored and they withdrew (the Clovelly lifeboat was then a pulling boat – rowed with oars). A large salvage tug also arrived, hoping for the contract to save the ship, but it also left when it became clear that the *Taxiarchis* was holed in several places.

The 'Taxiarchis' aground below Halfway Wall and severely holed

Felix Gade describes in *My Life on Lundy* how he and his team spent 24 hours without a break standing by to fire lines across to the ship to winch the crew to safety. Eventually a partial evacuation of the crew was authorised, and they brought off sixteen men. They were accommodated for a night in the Hotel, and Rene Gade and other island women worked hard to feed them. The next day, the remaining crew, including the recalcitrant master, were winched ashore, and the following day the *Lerina* arrived with the Salvage Association surveyor and a representative of the ship's London agents on board.

The crew being brought ashore above Halfway Wall Bay

The surveyor declared the *Taxiarchis* to be a total wreck, which meant that all the crew should immediately be taken to the mainland – a decision which was a relief to the islanders, especially the women who had been housing and feeding a crowd of men who spoke little or no English and whose appreciation of British conventions on hygiene was rudimentary.

Some of the crew of the 'Taxiarchis' safely landed by the rocket life saving team

Mr Gade wrote to MCH on 2 April:

> I expect you have heard through the newspapers of our latest wreck.
>
> Another Greek steamer ran ashore within 100 yards of where the "Maria Kyriakides" went ashore. I know you will be proud to hear that your Rocket Life Saving Company, numbering 5 men (the usual crew is 20 to 22) stuck to their job continuously for 72 hours and eventually landed the entire crew of 24 men and a ship's cat (male). Without wishing to brag, I must say that I think we have done well. The weather conditions were worse than bad. Strong easterly gales, with heavy and icy rain showers. We were on for 24 hours without a break and from then onwards at intervals for a further 48 hours. The lifeboats came from Clovelly and Appledore, stayed for about 8 hours and left the crew to their fate. Tugs came and went, giving it up as a bad job, but the Lundy crew stuck it out and did their job and did it well.
>
> The men, Charlie Smaldon, Jack Crews, Jack Bament and Sam Stookes deserve all the praise you can give them, and the women of the island, from Rene to Sam's wife, all did their bit, if it was only bringing out food for us. Don't overlook the fact that farm animals had to be fed and tended, just the same as if there was no wreck, and us in the middle of the lambing season too.
>
> I say for certain that if it had not been for us the whole crew would have perished, because no lifeboat could have lived in the seas which were running when we took the last 9 men off, and it would have been precarious to say the least of it for a boat to come alongside when we took the first 16 men off.
>
> I daresay you know that the B. of T. [Board of Trade] pay £1 per man for those saved and as you have taken over the Rocket apparatus you are responsible for this payment. Whether you can recover from the Underwriters or Owners I am unable to say, but it is possible.

CREW REFUSE TO ESCAPE

SHIP IMPALED BELOW TOWERING CLIFFS

From Our Own Correspondent
BARNSTAPLE, Sunday.

Though facing death, the crew of the 3,000 tons Greek steamer, Taxiarchis, refused to leave their ship when she ran ashore on Lundy Island last night in very bad and foggy weather.

Rockets were fired and breeches buoy communication was established with the ship.

The Appledore lifeboat also got alongside but, with a German tug standing by, the crew decided to remain on board.

"The steamer may break up. The men on board know it. But they want to stay until the last moment. They are good men," was the verdict of one of the lifeboat crew.

"She lies impaled in a dangerous spot under the towering cliffs of the island," the lifeboatman added.

"The tug which it is hoped will drag her off the rocks must wait for a change in the weather. This may come to-morrow, or in several days' time. Meantime the crew and their ship are in extreme danger."

The steamer, owned by Mr. C. M. Lemos, Chios, Greece, was outward bound from Liverpool and Barry, and had left port only a few hours.

From the 'Daily Herald',
30 March 1931

The incident did have the traditional longer-term advantages. The ship had been loaded with 6,000 tons of coal in South Wales and was bound for Rio de Janeiro when she struck Lundy. She was also carrying cans of olive oil and a good quantity of cigarettes, Greek and American, which could not be taken away to the mainland without paying duty, since they were duty-free for use on the voyage. It was quite some time before solid fuel had to be brought across to Lundy, and the smokers on the island had a range of new experiences for a while.

Amy Ruth Harman

MRS HARMAN had been in poor health for some time, and Mr Gade wrote: 'Late in 1930 all … had been concerned to hear of the grave deterioration in the health of Martin's charming wife, Amy. She was ordered to go to Madeira, but when she returned she was really no better.' She died in July of 1931.

Ruth and Diana were sent to Lundy with their governess, who had the heart-wrenching task of telling them of their mother's death. A few days later she was brought for burial in a coffin of white basket-work, lined with sweet-smelling hay from the paddocks of Burraland (near Uckfield, Sussex, where the Harmans lived). Everybody attended the service in the church, and a bugler sounded the last post before she was buried in the ancient cemetery.

Mr Harman chose a large piece of granite to cover the whole length of the grave, and one of the keepers at the South Light cut the inscription: Amy Ruth, wife of Martin Coles Harman. Born 13th August 1884. Died 28th July 1931. Ruth and Diana later had bronze plaques made for their parents' graves as the granite inscriptions had weathered.

Mrs Harman had gracefully fulfilled her role on Lundy, and she was most sincerely mourned. It must have been a very terrible time for MCH. Apart from his grief, he was fighting the grave consequences of the financial crash in 1929 that led to his bankruptcy.

THE FINANCIAL CRASH in 1929 brought disaster to MCH. By 1932 he was bankrupt, as the result of a judgement against him of one of the companies that had been under his management. He was sentenced to three years imprisonment, although he had not committed any criminal offence.

It was a very harsh experience, since none of the companies for which he was responsible came to grief, and he had been able to prevent their collapse.

Until that point, he had spent £15,000 on improvements on Lundy. Fortunately, he had earlier put the ownership of Lundy into a trust for his four children, so it was safe from being sold to pay his creditors.

Lundy lodgers

IN ADDITION to improving the hotel facilities (see page 50), MCH encouraged visitors to Lundy by leasing some properties, predominantly to tenants who wished to enjoy frequent or lengthy visits. The terms were that:

- Rents should be paid in cash on the island.
- No income tax communications whatsoever should be sent from, or addressed to, Lundy.
- No radios, guns or dogs to be kept.
- The tenant should 'maintain the historic immunities and privileges of Lundy'.
- The tenant may not sub-let.
- The owner may terminate a tenancy with one month's notice.
- The lease falls if the rent is overdue by more than 14 days.
- In the case of interpreting the agreement, the owner's written opinion is binding.

For some properties the tenant was to be responsible for repairs; for others a proportion of the costs was specified.

Tibbets as it appeared in 1951. It was built as a observation base by the Admiralty in 1911. When war was declared in 1914, it was fully fitted out as a war watching station with accommodation for four men. There was a watchtower on the roof, and a kitchen and washroom were built in a small corrugated iron hut on the east side. A signal pole was erected, and the whole site was contained within railings to exclude animals

Tibbets was leased for £12 per year to a London lawyer, Mr Smith Savile and his wife. The Cliff Bungalow (now Hanmers) was let at £25, and the Garden Bungalow (now Brambles) was let long-term. The watch room at Coastguard Cottages and the adjoining room were let to a geologist, Dr John Dollar, for £1 per year, who kept his equipment there. His brother, Ivor, rented the flag house at the Castle for 10s. a year.

The Garden Bungalow – now replaced by Bramble Villa – in 1953. Outside the door are Eva Zoref and Myrtle Langham

Miss Wilda Gee outside the Cliff Bungalow

Lundy attracted individualists. The tenant of the schoolhouse was Mrs Fotheringham, who was given notice – under protest – as she had made her income tax return from Lundy. Miss Gee, who was tenant of the Cliff Bungalow thought it her duty to raise the intellectual awareness of the islanders by inviting them to tea for readings from Dickens or Hardy, when they found it hard to try to keep straight faces. However, she was of resolute character; she survived a fall down Lone Pine Gulch and bravely climbed up again, and she had been an active suffragette.

An early view of Millcombe House from Diana Keast's album. The render was grey, not today's white; there was creeper on the wall; there was a porch, and there are no 'flanking' walls – both alterations made later by the Landmark Trust

The Harman family naturally occupied the Villa, and christened it Millcombe, which was furnished when they took it over. They ate their meals at the hotel, so there was a 'top table' in the dining room, where they were usually joined by Mr Gade and any guests who might be invited to join them. It could be convivial.

Millcombe House from above, showing the inward-sloping roof which was designed to catch rainwater. The 'Lerina' is anchored in the Landing Bay

The Hanmer family

M R GADE recalls the Hanmer family in *My Life on Lundy*. Starting in 1930, the Hanmer family, mother, father, six children and two maids, spent six weeks of every summer on Lundy for seven or eight years at a peppercorn rent. In return both Ruth and Diana were to be 'hardened off', so that they became resourceful, self-reliant, and uninhibited, ready to take their places at boarding school.

On arrival at the Old Light the children were sent out to cut and carry bracken to make their own mattresses. Mr Hanmer was the only one allowed a chair; the others had to scrounge boxes or beer crates on which to sit for meals. Everyone bathed nude at 6.30-7.00 each morning. After breakfast the children were provided with dry bread and a bar of chocolate each and told not to show their faces again until supper time. The young Hanmers were always hungry. '... we were dumbfounded at the amount those children consumed at mealtimes ... Every week a hamper of vegetables, fruit and eggs was sent from their Sussex garden.' Pa Hanmer's sole activity was fishing.

Above: Mrs Ivy Hanmer. On Lundy she was known as Peta

Left: The Hanmers at the Old Light

> The spaniel wasn't reliable and even bit the Hanmer children while guarding his mistress – entering the Old Light could be hazardous. I remember seeing the R101 airship when Nicky Hanmer and I were taken to the beach early one morning. Mr and Mrs Hanmer were Irish and had strong accents.

Bathing party at the Cove. Hanmers and Harmans with Felix Gade, left, and Rene Gade with her arms around Moyra Hanmer

When the Hanmers could not use the Old Light, the family took a lease of what was then called the Cliff Bungalow. The lease was paid regularly, even during the war when it could not be used. To acknowledge Mrs Hanmer's generosity, Felix Gade and Diana decided to call the newly-renovated Cliff Bungalow 'Hanmers' in 1962, and were rather disappointed that this did not call forth any response apart from one visit by Nicholas, his wife and child. By this time the family were all adults, and spread in their various careers.

Below, left to right: Daphne, Deny, Moyra and Paddy Hanmer. Daphne died of polio, aged 19

Mary Gade

MARY GADE, the daughter of Felix and Rene Gade, was born on 27 May 1933. Although her mother went to Bideford for the delivery, they were back on Lundy when Mary was 18 days old. Her father described her as 'as near to being a Lundy-born baby as any within the past fifty years.'

Right: Felix and Rene Gade with their daughter, Mary Ann Elizabeth, at her christening on 10 August 1933 at St Helen's Church. With them are Mary's godparents, Mary Wicksteed (later Countess Tolstoy-Miloslavsky) and David Clifford

Below left: Mary Gade and Diana Harman, probably in 1935

Below right: Mary in 1937

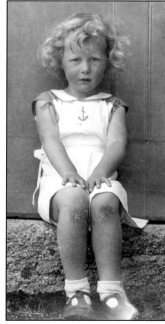

This delightful portrait of Mary Gade, then aged three years, was made by Ivor Dollar in 1936. It appeared in his collection of poems called *Solitudes*, and incorporates a charming view of her Lundy environment.

Ivor Dollar, like his brother, John, was a frequent visitor to Lundy, for which he had a deep and poetic affection. For some time he rented the flag house at the Castle, where he could camp in (rather than out) and store his belongings.

And in that blaze of golden light, where sea and sun and sky combine, there floats ... a shade that is a world apart, a link dropped from the chain of Time – an island hung in ageless space.

LUNDY

Ivor Dollar's drawing of the church and village – with some artistic licence – which appeared in 'Solitudes'

'Solitudes' bears the dedication: To "Giant", "Cheerful" and the Lundy Nymphs

Steamers and teas

IN THE HOLIDAY SEASON the Campbell steamers would bring considerable numbers of day trippers to Lundy from Wales and Ilfracombe. All hands were busily employed on 'boat days'. Such visits could not be compared with those of today; the trippers took tea in the 'Tea Room' (a corrugated-iron building where the Black Shed now stands), or crowded through the one door to the tavern and small shop, struggled to get a drink and their postcards, and then emerged to see what there was to be seen: the farm, the Church and the Old Lighthouse. Resident visitors, friends of the islanders, would very often help in the bar, the tea room, and in the shop. They would also sometimes set up a postcard table outside, to ease the crush in the tiny shop with its narrow doorway.

Right: standing by to welcome boarders. Felix Gade on a boat day, with two 1930s paddle steamers in the Landing Bay

Below: and here they come ...

At first there were no guide books, or books about the island. If the sun shone it would be beautiful, but in bad weather they may well have wondered why they had come. The compensation was that there were no licensing hours ...

Trippers were ferried back to the steamer for the return journey a few at a time in small launches. On very busy days a queue would grow but people were understanding and patient. At peak times, in good weather, 700 trippers might be landed.

Queuing to return to the steamer. This photo, taken in 1969, shows the path and steps from the quay to the south lighthouse. On the far left, on Cove Beach, is the slipway, built during the Christie ownership (1918-25). To reach it, another way down was made from the lighthouse, but perhaps not one for the fainthearted

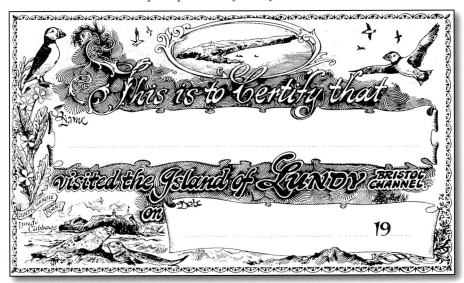

A 'Visitor's Certificate', produced by John Dyke in 1974 and sold as a postcard

Lundy has travel by air

WITH THE ESTABLISHMENT of Heanton Court Airfield, near Barnstaple, and the formation of Barnstaple & North Devon Air Services in 1933, it was quickly seen that this offered a new and exciting possibility of an air service to Lundy. A provisional licence was obtained for the Lundy airfield, which consisted of a runway (rough grassland) east-west across Acland's Moor (now called the Airfield). The first passengers were landed on 2 and 3 June 1934. Unfortunately one of the planes was subsequently damaged on landing and was taken back to the mainland on the *Lerina*. However, the runway was extended by the demolition of a section of the north-south wall that divided the airfield, and flights were resumed.

De Havilland Dragon, G-ACCR, on the airfield before its mishap. Left to right are: Bob Boyd (pilot), Felix Gade, Hector Munro, ?, ?, Bob Helson (with cap), ?, Stanley Smith, ?, Charlie Smaldon

The fuselage of G-ACCR athwart two boats for transportation out to the 'Lerina'

The air service was of great importance to Lundy, not least to MCH because it greatly reduced the time taken to get to the island from London. The fast overnight train from London to Barnstaple would give time for an early flight to Lundy – that is, wind, weather and the vagaries of the pilot willing.

That the post bag was carried by plane meant that there was an airmail service, and Lundy stamps were produced accordingly, though the early airmail labels shown here were issued by the airline and are not true Lundy stamps.

Two early airmail labels

Lundy's airmail service in action. This is a later, post-war, aircraft. On the left is the pilot, Maurice Looker, and Frank Cannon is handling the mail bags

Family holidays: the growing children

Martin Coles Harman and his four children on Lundy in 1935. At the back are John (left) and Albion (right), and in front are Ruth, MCH and Diana

In the Hotel garden in 1933. Rear, left to right: Wyndham Clifford, Mary Wicksteed, Sheila Hanmer, John Harman, Felix Gade, Diana Harman on his shoulders, Dick Ayres (Trinity House), Paddy Hanmer. Front, left to right: ?, Geoff Leader, Nicky Hanmer, Ruth Harman, Roy White, Jan Aylen, Rene Gade

Left: Albion at Easter 1932 showing off a conger eel which he had caught with a borrowed boathook in the hold of the wrecked 'Taxiarchis'. Right: John enjoying farmyard chores. Diana remembers that he was in charge of the chickens but could be absent-minded. It was not rare to find a nest in the gorse which had escaped his attention with twenty eggs in it

What had been a place for a small horse-drawn trap alongside stables for the Heaven family became a sales stall for the younger Harman generation during their holidays. They assiduously collected white heather which was sold in small bundles to the trippers, along with model puffins, as they made their way up from the steamer. The gate up to Millcombe – marked 'Private' – is on the right

On the Landing Beach. Left: Ruth, Diana, Albion (photo taken c.1934 by Mrs Hanmer).
Right: John

On the Landing Beach: Albion

Tubby Harrison

COLONEL R.N. 'TUBBY' HARRISON first came to Lundy with the 99th Bristol Cabot Sea Scouts for their camping holiday in 1927. Some thirty boys stayed for a fortnight, when they enjoyed Lundy to the utmost. One whole day was marked off to be devoted to Lundy work, but the boys were keen, and were rounding up sheep, discharging the *Lerina*, helping in the tea room, washing up, mowing lawns, and filling gaps in dry stone walls. In addition they presented a variety show for the general entertainment. It was huge success, and the Scouts paid annual visits for several following years.

After his retirement, Tubby was able to spend much of his time on Lundy, and he rented the School Bungalow (now usually called the Blue Bung). In honour of the extent of his famous hospitality, the islanders soon christened it 'The Red Lion'. Tubby was always ready and very willing to join in any work or entertainment and he arranged fine parties for Mrs Gade's birthday (11 September). He was an early enthusiast for cine film; he shot extensive footage of his journey from Bristol to Lundy on the steamer and documented all aspects of Lundy life. He put on film shows when he was on Lundy.

Home-made poster announcing a showing of Tubby Harrison's cine film

Tubby Harrison died in 1952, and his ashes were brought to Lundy and scattered in front of his 'Red Lion'. Much to general disappointment, his films disappeared without trace until old reels of film were found many years later when a Bristol undertaker's premises were being cleared. One of the company recognised Lundy, and the film found its way to the drama department of Bristol University who have a post-graduate course in film and television studies. They made contact with Diana. An international group of students processed what could be saved, and became so interested that they went to Lundy and filmed a delightful small portrait of the island which combined selected footage from the original films with modern scenes and interviews recorded on Lundy and elsewhere with many people who know Lundy well. The resulting film, *A Little Kingdom*, was nominated for a Royal Television Society factual award in 2008.

DEATH OF ALDERMAN R. N. HARRISON

A lover of Lundy

BRISTOL lost one of its best known and most colourful personalities yesterday, when the death occurred suddenly, at his home of Alderman Robert Norman Harrison, a member of the City Council for over 16 years.

Above: a still from 'A Little Kingdom', showing some of Tubby Harrison's original footage very well restored by the Bristol team. This shot is of the 'Red Lion'

Left: part of Tubby's obituary in the Bristol 'Evening Post' of 13 February 1952

Some islanders in 1932, in a photo taken by John Dollar. Left to right: Joan Roberts, Rene Smaldon in front, Mrs Roberts, Jackie Smaldon in front, Maggie Smaldon with baby, Elsie Smaldon, Felix Gade, Diana Harman and dog in front, Tom Hill, Jack Crews, Charlie Smaldon, Rene Gade (and dog)

Some islanders in 1936. Back row, left to right: Stanley Smith, farmhand with Joan Crews, D. Lang (fisherman), Jack Crews, Bill Bowling (South Light). Front row, left to right: ?, Chick Evans (cart man), Alf Orchard (fisherman), Bob Helson

The *Carmine Filomena*

HE MORNING of 2 July 1937 was very foggy. When the fog cleared it was seen that a steamer had struck near Rat Island. It was the *Carmine Filomena*, of Genoa, laden with a cargo of Welsh coal. The captain put his hopes on tugs, but when a powerful tug was summoned and made several attempts to pull the vessel free, it had no effect at all. The position was complicated because the ship was on the tide race at the south-east corner of the island. The Salvage Association's ship, the *Ranger*, was sent to Lundy as it was thought possible that the ship and the cargo might be salvaged.

The captain of the *Carmine Filomena* rented a cottage for his crew, except for those it was necessary to keep on board. The salvage people decided to discharge the cargo; the *Ranger*'s bunkers were topped up, and then Mr Gade had the painful experience of watching tons of beautiful coal being tipped into the sea. When he remonstrated that the coal would be very useful to Lundy the *Ranger* captain offered to sell it to him, though it was not his to sell. Eventually a boat-load of coal was given in exchange for some lobsters, but the *Ranger* captain systematically destroyed many items that could have been of good use to Lundy, possibly because he was used to taking all the wreck goods for himself.

Meanwhile the crew of the wrecked ship had given much appreciated help with the harvest. Eventually the wreck began to break up and the *Ranger* took the crew to Ilfracombe. To use Mr Gade's description: 'We came into our own. We had everything off that ship in three days, including a couple of lifeboats.'

The 'Carmine Filomena' aground off Rat Island

Richard Perry: an early ornithologist

IN THE SPRING of 1939, Richard Perry went with his wife to stay in Stoneycroft, as Lundy was 'the only place ... where I might watch colonial nesting sea birds comparatively undisturbed.' He stayed for five months, concentrating on the cliff study of Guillemots, Puffins, Razorbills and Kittiwakes, mostly at the North End. They very much enjoyed Lundy and the people they knew there, although the cottage, 'with its crumbling discoloured walls and bare floors, its leaking roof, smoking chimney and icy drafts ... was less habitable than any shepherd's croft in the Western Isles.'

Richard Perry and his wife at Stoneycroft in summer 1939

Perry wrote of Lundy's 'boundless spaciousness and the mental exhilaration of the pure air and untrammelled freedom, which on calm days ... made me instinctively and physically at one with nature.' His book is a delight, beautifully written, and the very excellent photographs were taken by Alan Richardson of Crediton, who, sadly, was killed in Tunisia in 1943.

Left: guillemots nesting on Devil's Chimney. Below: 'The puffin was to make a stronger appeal to me than any other bird.' All photos on this page by Alan Richardson

Lundy at war

IN THE LAST FEW DAYS of August 1939 it became obvious that a declaration of war was imminent, and visitors to Lundy made preparations to leave with the Campbell steamer that was due to arrive on 1 September. It proved to be the last for ten years. In July of 1940 the *Lerina* was commandeered by the Admiralty, which undertook to convey islanders, stores and supplies, though visitors would only be carried by special permission of the Senior Naval Officer at Appledore. Freight was charged at ten shillings (50p) per ton, and passengers a return fare of ten shillings. It sounds drastic – as it was – but the naval authorities came to be considerate and helpful in exercising their powers, although at the outset Albion and Diana were refused passage, which was very upsetting as Lundy was their home. Mary Gade was taken to and brought from school in Bideford, accompanied by her father, and Dr Dollar later wangled a passage – although he might well have claimed to be on war business as he was deputed by MCH to identify island sources of molybdenum for war supplies. This he did, but good relations came to an end, as he charged MCH for his services, despite having received much consideration and some privileges on the island.

Early in 1940 a Royal Navy War Watching Station was installed at the Old Light, which was leased to the Admiralty, and the radio telephone installation was taken over. The crew there consisted of a lieutenant, a C.P.O. and five ratings. Mr H. Catchpole was in command during the whole of the war and in 1944 was raised to a Lt Commander. His relationship with Mr and Mrs Gade became a very cordial and mutually supportive friendship.

The workforce for the island farm was provided by Jock Robertson, who was excluded from army service as he was disabled by the loss of one hand, although he proved capable of caring for the sheep and shearing them. A series of five land girls was sent, of whom Mr Gade remarked that two were really good. For the girls, it must surely have counted as a hardship post.

At the end of 1940 Mr Harman sent a Mr Van Os and his people to take over a ten-year lease for which, strangely, there was no fee or rent. Mr and Mrs Gade moved to Millcombe and all the other employees left the island. Mr Gade was bitterly opposed to this arrangement and he never had a good word for Van Os or his misdoings. But one thing that was achieved was the arrival of the first mechanised vehicle on Lundy. This was a Fordson 24 h.p. tractor which had been allowed by the Ministry of Agriculture, according to Mr Gade, on Van Os's plea that it was needed to bring about an increase in food production for the war effort (although the War Agricultural Committee had not scheduled Lundy for war production). In the event, the extra acres were not ploughed, but until then all the heavy work on the farm, and all the haulage, had been carried out with a small team of horses.

Most of the island men joined up, and those four remaining constituted a unit of the Home Guard. A senior officer was sent over to inspect the members of the Home Guard, although Mr Gade was the only member there at the time, and this poor officer was very severely seasick on his passage to the island. When he was sufficiently

The new Fordson tractor on the Landing Beach in 1941

recovered, he inspected Mr Gade's uniform and equipment – which did not include any ammunition for small arms – before he had to face the return journey. The Lundy Home Guard – amazingly – proved to be the only one to meet the enemy face to face.

On 3 March 1941 a German Heinkel bomber crash-landed to the south of Halfway Wall. The first news Felix Gade had of it was when seven-year-old Mary burst into his office saying 'There's a Jerry plane, and it's coming down.' The crew survived and

Lighthouse Keeper Reg Guppy at the wreckage of the Heinkel He 111 in 1941

immediately set fire to the plane, and said that they had been forced to land because of mechanical trouble. As they had no bomb load, it was obvious that they were returning from a bombing raid. They handed over their weapons and were taken into custody at the Old Light by the naval detachment there, until the Royal Navy arrived to take them as prisoners to the mainland.

The engine of the plane remained for some time *in situ,* but piece by piece has been dismantled as many people have been unable to resist taking a souvenir. Now less remains to be seen. Fifty years later, in 1991, Elmar Bötcher, the plane's navigator, returned to Lundy and enjoyed a meeting of mutual cordiality.

An engine of the 'Halfway Wall' Heinkel He 111 photographed in 1968.
Less remains today, though the site can still be found

It was not surprising that first reports of a second German plane coming down on Lundy less than a month later were greeted with scepticism, especially since the date was 1 April. But another He 111 had indeed crashed into the west sideland and was burning furiously. Two of the crew were killed but three survived, one badly injured. They, too, were taken prisoner by the R.N. detachment at the Old Light and moved to Appledore – where only firm action by the military authorities prevented them from being attacked by local people who believed that they were responsible for the machine-gunning of a fishing boat, the *Kestrel.* The mate was killed and the surviving crew spent several days on Lundy after the attack.

A third aircraft crashed on 1 June 1942, this time, unfortunately, an RAF Whitley bomber returning to Chivenor from anti-submarine patrol over the Bay of Biscay. All the crew were killed, and the body of the tail-gunner was retrieved by John Pennington Harman. A framed memorial to the crew is now on display in the window of the Office.

In other respects, normal life went on. Members of the family came for summer holidays and for Christmas celebrations. Albion Harman had married Kathleen (Kay) Bloxam on 2 September 1939, the day before war was declared. Ruth married Peter Jones – they adopted the surname Harman Jones – in June 1940, and Diana and Kenneth Keast were married in August 1942.

Above: a relaxed tea-picnic at the Cove in the long, hot summer of 1940. Left to right: Mary Gade (asleep), Diana Harman, Ken Keast (back to camera), Felix Gade, Rene Gade

Left: Ruth Harman Jones and Ken Keast at Millcombe at Christmas 1941

> Clothes were sent over in the war from America. We had a trunk of American clothes distributed by Missions to Seamen, but they were quite unsuitable. However, both Ken and Cheerful were great ones for theatre, and that became our dressing-up box. The trunk was in the cellar at Millcombe for a long time.

John Pennington Harman, V.C.

TRAGIC NEWS reached Martin Coles Harman in the spring of 1944. His elder son, John, had been sent with his regiment, the Fourth Battalion of the Queen's Own Royal West Kent Regiment, to fight the Japanese, who had invaded the area of Kohima at the Burma/India border. There he lost his life in a very gallant action, for which he was awarded a posthumous Victoria Cross.

Conditions there were very tough. The battle site was described by Captain Peter Dorosa: the garrison was outnumbered and under severe pressure from the Japanese, who for two weeks 'kept up a relentless bombardment, and sniper fire, with mass charges – screaming and blowing bugles.'[*] The garrison was not of sufficient strength to make a counter-attack, and John took a lone action upon himself:

John P. Harman's passport photograph, taken in Auckland, New Zealand, in July 1939

His citation reads:

> At Kohima, Assam, on 8th April 1944, Lance Corporal Harman was commanding a section of a forward platoon. The enemy had established a machine-gun post within 50 yards of his position which became a serious menace to the remainder of his company. Unable to bring the fire of his section on to the post, Lance Corporal Harman went forward by himself and annihilated the post, returning with the enemy machine-gun. The next morning, having first recovered a forward position, he again charged an enemy post alone, shooting four and bayonetting one, thereby wiping out the post. As he returned Lance Corporal Harman received a burst of machine-gun fire in his side and died shortly after reaching our lines. Lance Corporal Harman's heroic action and supreme devotion to duty were largely responsible for the decisive way in which all attacks were driven off by his company.

His last words were, 'I got the lot. It was worth it.'

MCH later presented the V.C. to John's regiment. He planned a memorial to be placed in the church on Lundy, but the ecclesiastical authorities wanted to make a change in the wording. MCH was incensed, and decided to establish a memorial in what is now V.C. Quarry. As a result of this dispute, no funeral service was held for him in the church after his death in 1954.

---

[*] By kind permission of the *Daily Telegraph*. Obituary of Captain Peter Dorosa, 3 April 2012

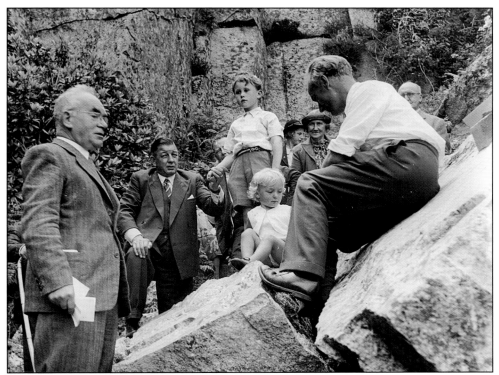

The unveiling of the memorial to John Pennington Harman, V.C., in what is now called V.C. Quarry on 20 June 1949. On the left is Martin Coles Harman; on the right is Albion Harman. The children are Martin Harman Jones and John Albion Harman. Mrs Laramy, housekeeper at Millcombe before the war, is between Albion and the children. Her husband had been the island farmer, and her son had also been killed in the war

The memorial reads:

Greater love hath no man than this,
That a man lay down his life for his friends
To the memory of
JOHN PENNINGTON HARMAN
aged 29
son of
Martin Coles Harman and Amy Ruth Harman
who died of wounds in Burma on
Easter Sunday the ninth of April 1944
For his bravery he was awarded the
VICTORIA CROSS
This tablet is erected by his brother and sisters
Albion Pennington Harman
Ruth Pennington Harman Jones
Diana Pennington Keast
At the going down of the sun and in the morning we will remember them

The Quarry memorial was an inspired choice: a fitting place for a proud memorial to honour a son of Lundy for all time.

A more intimate moment after the unveiling: MCH, Albion, John and Martin.
This photograph and the one on the previous page are © R.L. Knight Ltd, Barnstaple

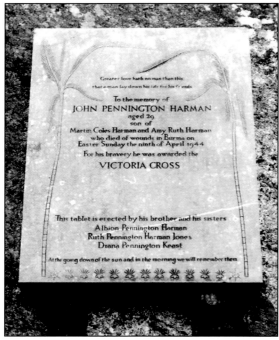

The memorial plaque before it weathered, showing the betel nut palm decoration

Statuette of John Pennington Harman, V.C., which was cast from some of the regimental silver when the Royal West Kents were disbanded in 1961

The Victoria Cross and campaign medals awarded posthumously to L/Cpl Harman are now in the keeping of the Queens' Own Royal West Kent Regiment Museum, Maidstone.

This replica Victoria Cross and duplicate campaign medals which are on display in the Tavern were purchased by Warrant Officer P.R. Doughty ATC and presented to Lundy by No. 1404 (Chatham) Squadron, Air Training Corps on behalf of Kent Wing, Air Training Corps and Kent branches of the Burma Star Association on 18 February 1990

The grave of John Pennington Harman at the Commonwealth War Graves cemetery at Kohima

Watercolour by John Dyke of the 50th anniversary service at V.C. Quarry on 23 June 1994 showing Marion Evans (née Harman Jones) and her daughter, Bronwen

The Lundy Field Society: early years

MARTIN COLES HARMAN was the first to see and to value Lundy for its qualities of natural beauty, peace and quiet, and to find the wealth of bird life to be a source of delight and interest. It was his purpose to guard all these with care, and to build up interest in the wildlife of the island in harmony with the habitat.

He was a keen bird watcher, which was shown in the publication of his two papers in British Birds in 1943: *The Hoopoe on Lundy* and *The First Breeding of the Fulmar in the South-West*. Unlike many of his predecessors, he had no interest in shooting as a sport, nor in the exploitation of the massive deposits of birds' eggs in season.

In 1945 the committee of the Devon Birdwatching and Preservation Society discussed the bird ringing stations that had been established in the Isles of Scilly and the islands of Skomer and Skokholm (Pembrokeshire) for the study of bird migration, and it was suggested that a station on Lundy could provide a very interesting link to these. Leslie Harvey, a lecturer in the Zoology department of what is now Exeter University, was appointed to write to Mr Harman to enquire whether a Lundy station might be possible, where the members could set up a Heligoland trap and ringing station, and compile studies for publication. Having established that this would be a concern exclusive to Lundy, and that the members would respect 'the island's peculiar rights and privileges', Mr Harman responded with enthusiasm. He was pleased to approve a Lundy Bird-watching Committee, and to be the first subscriber to the funds with a generous gift of £50. Also, on application, members intending to stay on the island would be given invitations from the owner that would exempt them from payment of the landing fee of one shilling. Harman approved the Constitution of the Committee, that now became the Lundy Field Society (LFS), and accepted the invitation to be its first President. Mr Harman was also very generous in giving the Society the use of the splendid Old Lighthouse for a headquarters and a hostel, and the members worked hard to get it ready for use.

Sketches of Leslie Harvey and Martin Coles Harman on a postcard to mark the fiftieth anniversary of the Lundy Field Society. The Old Light headquarters is also shown in this drawing by John Dyke

Leslie Harvey summed up those early days:

> I well remember my first, critical, correspondence with him in January 1946. I wrote to an unknown to ask whether he would consider the idea of a group of naturalists going to his island in order to study its natural history. His reply was only mildly encouraging, as well it might be. But it was not actively discouraging, and upon my being able to reassure him that we had no designs on the ancient integrity of Lundy I received a letter so generous and warm as to assure me that our about-to-be-born society had a certain future. Among four conditions laid down, the second was: *The said Committee to be formed at my suggestion herein made; I to be the first subscriber to its fund in the sum of £50 hereby promised.*
>
> After that all was plain sailing; a group of us interested in the idea met in Exeter and discussed ways and means, sent an exploratory expedition to Lundy in June, and by the end of the summer the Lundy Field Society was in existence, born through Mr Harman's vigour and vision, out of the Devon Bird-Watching and Preservation Society. By the following spring we had been given free use of the Old Lighthouse, and were able to see our way towards maintaining a warden in permanent charge. All this was no light matter, particularly in those years immediately following the end of the war, and it was due very largely to Mr Harman's advice, encouragement and help that we succeeded. From that time onwards, I, as Secretary, was to find him an everlasting source of delight and strength. Sometimes things happened which he didn't like, and he wrote immediately to say so, but in terms which caused no offence but only the wish to put things right. That we always arrived, swiftly, at an amicable conclusion was due in no small measure to his friendliness and his readiness to see a point of view. At other times he was pleased with something, particularly when we obtained a new record for Lundy, and again he wrote to me immediately to say so.

By the time of the first AGM in 1947 the Society had appointed a warden, who was responsible for bird observations and for running the hostel (on a minimal budget). There was a membership of 127, who paid subscriptions of 7s. 6d. per year, and 38 of whom had stayed at the somewhat Spartan hostel in its first year. The Annual Report lists observations of 97 species of birds as well as other work: altogether a praiseworthy achievement, at a time when transport to the island was problematical, food rationing was still in force and some materials were in short supply.

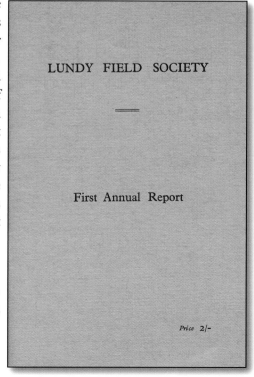

LUNDY FIELD SOCIETY

First Annual Report

Price 2/-

The first Annual Report of the Lundy Field Society, for the year 1947, produced in drab, post-war style. The Secretary is listed as Leslie Harvey, and the Treasurer was Rosemary Studdy, who wrote the first post-war guide book to Lundy in 1949 (see the pictorial map on page 5)

In each of the succeeding reports Mr Harman wrote an interesting 'owner's letter', giving his ideas and opinions on island matters, information, advice and encouragement. He was full of ideas for island activities that show that he was very much aware of the pleasures and the problems of his island, and that the help given by members in various island tasks was much appreciated, although they were also advised 'to get as much fun out of the place as you can.' He also took particular care to warn members of the need to wear robust footwear to prevent accidents.

Two John Dyke commentaries on the activities of the LFS. Left: 'A windy day at the Old Light' from the LFS Old Light log for 26 April 1957. Right: a good fug at the Old Light, a lovely vignette from the LFS second Annual Report

Left: the 'Garden Trap', a Heligoland Bird Trap built in 1949 over the wall from what is now Old Light Cottage (roof in foreground)

Right: the LFS built a much larger bird trap on the Quarry Terrace, a better location for catching birds, especially migrating birds in spring and autumn. The objective was for both recording and ringing. The 'Bird Hut', photographed in 1953, built against the north wall of the main Quarry Terrace, was where ringing was carried out. The Heligoland Trap on the Quarry Terrace is still there but the bird hut is long gone

Mr Harman's sudden death in 1954 was a heavy blow. Leslie Harvey wrote:

The debt which the Society owes to M. C. Harman is beyond telling. But it is for his personal qualities that I at least shall miss him most. He had an inexhaustible store of impish vitality which made every letter from him, every meeting with him, an event. He seemed to have retained his youthful capacity for excitement and adventure, and it manifested itself in his jealous guardianship of, and pride in, his small kingdom under the shadow of the larger Britain. Those who have been privileged to meet him on the soil of Lundy will remember vividly how happy he was there, walking through the bracken and heather to take stock of his Soay sheep, or deer, or golden orfe, calling at the Old Light to ask for news of birds passing through, shooting the deer to control their numbers, or the geese for Christmas dinners, or talking with knowledge and animation on some point of Lundy's history to some chance visitor in the bar of the Marisco. Always was he brimming with zest and pride in his realm. It was this that made Lundy so charming a place; for his benevolent autocracy brooked few of the restrictions which hem round our mainland lives. And so I shall always think of him as a king in his kingdom, proud and pleased when a Hoopoe, a roller, a Golden Oriole or, better still, an American Robin took brief sanctuary within his shores.

In honour of their president's memory, the LFS refurbished Old Light West as a laboratory for members working on their studies.

Old Light West, formerly the LFS laboratory and now accommodation for Landmark staff

COLLECTOR'S PERMIT.

IN AN EFFORT to curb egg-snatching and protect breeding birds, MCH designed this permit. It was over-optimistic to expect collectors to present themselves for inspection before leaving the island, so, sadly, this measure failed.

It is impossible to know what the loss of eggs may have been, but it underlines the obligations of visitors to respect the wishes of the owner.

The *Amstelstroom*

O N 17 JULY 1947, the Dutch coaster *Amstelstroom* ran aground on the west coast, just north of the Battery. Mr Gade was off the island at the time, and records in *My Life on Lundy* that he was informed that a Dutch seaman had arrived at the hotel that morning at breakfast time. He had climbed up the cliffs from where his ship was stuck fast between the rocks. A contemporary newspaper report says that the first to know of the wreck 'were birdwatchers in a disused lighthouse who were waiting for the fog to lift. They heard knocks on the door, and outside found the exhausted crew, soaked and their clothing in tatters'.

The *Amstelstroom* was a total wreck, but fortunately there was no loss of life, since Captain Jansen and the ten-man crew were able to get ashore and climb to the top of the island. The islanders looked after them, and made and kept contact with the Coastguard until the men could be taken off.

Later, MCH received a letter of thanks and appreciation for the help and care given to the crew, and for Lundy's efficiency in establishing and maintaining contact with the Coastguard.

The Dutch owners wrote to MCH, expressing a wish to do something to benefit the island, which he suggested might be repairs to the roof of the Rocket Shed, and a light trailer for carrying the life-saving equipment. With his reply, he enclosed a copy of his reprint of Steinman Steinman.

The Battery in 1920, when the gun house still had its roof. The 'Amstelstroom' was wrecked just to the right of this view. Inset: a lifebelt from the 'Amstelstroom' on display in the Tavern

Jim Prouse

O N THE RIGHT is Jim Prouse, with his dog, Jeanie. He came to Lundy from Hartland with Mr and Mrs Gade in 1949, when they returned to Lundy after illness. He ran the bar for many years – in the days when there were no closing hours, so that the barman's spell of duty could be very long, especially on Friday nights after pay-day.

Jeanie was a fine rabbiter, and during some very lean times, the rabbits she caught made a welcome contribution to managing on a very tight economy.

Jim assisted Mr Gade in preparing a grave for MCH in 1954. They were working against time, but it has to be recorded that three charges of explosives were used in the vicinity of the chapel, in what is now known to be a sixth century early Christian burial ground – but that was not dreamt of then.

Felix Gade speaks highly of Jim Prouse in *My Life on Lundy*: 'He always wore a white jacket during bar hours, and he made a practice of ringing the North or South Lighthouses to inform them when any of their number, or even any mechanics and labourers, left the Tavern to

return home. Mr Gade goes on to recount a man 'missing' on his way home to the South Light who was eventually found by Jim Prouse – in the wee small hours, after he had been woken up to make a search – sleeping it off in the porch of the back door of Millcombe House.

Jim Prouse in his natural habitat – the old Tavern – in 1955

Post-war paddle-steamers and planes

CAMPBELL'S STEAMERS re-started services to Lundy after the war on 20 June 1949 – which is why that date was decided upon for the dedication of the memorial plaque to John Pennington Harman in V.C. Quarry (see page 94). Air services resumed in 1950, though run by different companies.

De Havilland Rapide, G-AKNY, loading luggage and passengers. Mr Gade is supervising, top right, and Leslie Harvey of the LFS is on the left, with his perpetual pipe. Diana remembers Mr Drabble, the doughty war-time pilot, would complain 'too much bloody luggage' as he struggled to get airborne

Arriving in 1952 in the Auster, G-AJXC, are (left to right) MCH, the Revd Hugh Muller, Maurice Looker (the pilot) and Canon Buttle. This aircraft also appears on page 81, carrying the mails

The Lundy Field Society: new wardens, tragedy and triumph

I N SEPTEMBER 1951 Peter Davis took over as LFS warden from David Lea and, like his predecessor, he was both well-liked and an assiduous ornithologist. In October 1952 Mary Gade reported to him that she had sighted a very unusual bird, which proved be an American Robin (*Turdus migratorius*), which was ringed before it left the island in November. The identification was accepted by the authorities and added to the British list, as detailed in *British Birds* of October 1953. MCH commented that this bird's migration was of around 3000 miles non-stop, during which it lost one-third of its weight.

Wendy Mitchell came from Mortehoe to work in the island shop for the 1952 season. She was pretty with lovely red hair, and she was very friendly. Soon she and Peter became engaged – a very happy event.

Then there was a tragic accident: while Peter was working on the rocks just south of Threequarter Wall, Wendy, who had been sitting above, suddenly lost her footing and fell to her death.

Wendy Mitchell had been an aspiring poet, and a memorial plaque to her was placed on one of the wooden benches on the east side. It contains a fragment of her verse. A similar memorial in stone can also be found on a rock on the west side near the spot where the tragedy happened.

'Where summer-long ...'.
One of the memorials to
Wendy Anne Mitchell

Understandably, Peter Davis did not stay on Lundy for much longer, and his successor is celebrated in the annals of the LFS. Barbara Whitaker (by profession a geologist) proved to be a warden of outstanding qualities. Firstly for her tireless diligence in recording her observations of the sightings and movements of birds, and ringing them. No less for her attention to record-keeping, and to fostering the interests of LFS members staying at the Old Light. There were no luxuries and few comforts in the hostel, but congenial company, with shared interests, and hot cocoa, characterised discussions round a good fire.

In 1955, American journalist and author, John Sack, visited a series of small and little-known territories and described them in a book called *Report from Practically Nowhere*. Lundy was first on his list. In an amused, amusing and perceptive piece, he notes: '... there surely hasn't been anything of such profound consequence to the average bird of Lundy as the founding of the Lundy Field Society there, in 1946. Since then, the birds have scarcely known a moment to call their own.' He met Barbara Whitaker at the Old Light, which was '... a perfect chaos: of tables and rickety orange crates, of dirty dishes, of unwrapped butter, marmalade tins, Spam cans, and dismembered bits of liverwurst and baloney, of shaggy gray-green books in topless heaps, of bulletin boards, broadsides and ornithological pin-ups, and, in the interstices of all this, moving guardedly, of Miss Whitaker and the bird watchers, all of them wearing baggy woolen sweaters and looking absolutely in the pink of health.'

'Since then, the birds have scarcely known a moment to call their own'. A cartoon by John
Teppich which appeared in Harper's Magazine in November 1956 to accompany a version
of John Sack's tale of his visit to Lundy

Barbara accounted for a more-than-usually-remarkable episode in LFS history. She made her way to Shutter Rock at the south-west point of the island, where she was carrying out a study of the shags' nests. To get there, she swam across some twenty yards from the base of the cliffs, but when she was ready to go back she found that she was cut off by storming seas. A company of islanders gathered, anxiously overlooking the Shutter. At last it was decided that as rescue was impossible, a rope line was thrown over, so that blankets and food could be sent by a pulley. She spent the night there, and the next day returned, with the comment that 'It was well worth it.' She had, naturally, not lost the opportunity of making fresh observations. There was a large gathering of islanders and visitors to oversee events, and the role of John Ogilvie in husbanding rescue operations will not be forgotten.

In October 1954, *Illustrated* magazine ('Every Wednesday – fourpence') had an article called 'Barbara of Bird Island'. The strapline: 'She turned down a plum job – for a £3-a-week life that needs a strong will, strong nerves and a strong stomach'. The story recounted Barbara's adventure on the Shutter and described her life as LFS warden with many colour and black and white photographs

Barbara with a juvenile shag. She did all her climbing in bare feet

Above: Barbara and Mary Haworth at work in the Old Light

Right: Barbara 'at home' in the Old Light. She's reading a bird book – all the books were bird books

Barbara left Lundy in 1956 to be married. Her departure was generally lamented, and Albion Harman wrote in the LFS Report that '... she has been a valued islander and all on Lundy wish her well in the future.'

Barbara and David Snow, Simla, Trinidad, c.1959. Source Dr A.E. ('Ted') Hill. David Snow was also an ornithologist; they both had distinguished careers in their field and did significant original research

'Operation Beef'

A CRISIS IN TRANSPORT arose towards the end of 1952, when the plane company went into liquidation – or, to put it more bluntly, ran out of money and suddenly ceased operation. Fortunately a new company was formed by members of the North Devon Flying Club, who restored the service with the Auster aircraft, and provided a very good service.

While passengers and smaller loads were brought over by air, this left the problem of the transport of coal, fuel, liquors and other heavy goods, but both the steamer company (P. & A. Campbell Ltd) and Trinity House were very supportive and most helpful in transporting heavy loads.

An exceptional exercise was carried out in February 1953 when it was necessary to reduce the number of cattle and ponies, and the money from their sale was much needed. There being no boat, the problem of transport was solved by the commander of the School of Combined Operations at Fremington Army Camp, who arranged for a tank landing craft to carry out an exercise to Lundy. The vessel came to the island, where it was a simple matter to lead the animals up the ramp to the hold of the vessel, and the exercise, which was christened 'Operation Beef', was a great success. Which was just as well, as the cost of insurance would have been prohibitive, and the only charge made was for £60. It was a field day for reporters and the press coverage ensured a good attendance at the auction; sales receipts for Lundy were £900.

Ponies and cattle – but, fortunately, no white horses that day

How Mr Gade found time for everything is a puzzle, but he did and was very seldom seen out of humour. He handled all the correspondence and the bookings for the hotel, supervised the ordering of supplies and the storage of carcases after a shoot, was responsible for running the farm and the island, and he handled the stamp business.

A Viking incursion

Aᴍ Mʀ J.S. Kɪɴɢ, an enthusiast of Norse history, was interested in the story of Eric Bloodaxe, a Viking invader. In 1953 he set up 'The Most Excellent Order of the Black Raven,' of which he was the 'Knight Commander', and Martin Coles Harman agreed to be 'Patron'. In a letter to a potential supporter, Mr King describes the purpose of the Order as being to explore and promote interest in the Scandinavian period of British History.

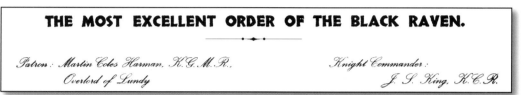

THE MOST EXCELLENT ORDER OF THE BLACK RAVEN.

Patron: Martin Coles Harman, K.G.M.R.,
Overlord of Lundy

Knight Commander:
J. S. King, K.C.R.

The letterhead of 'The Most Excellent Order of the Black Raven'

1954 was the one-thousandth anniversary of the death of Eric Bloodaxe, the last Norse king of York, and, by a progression that is now not clear, one result was the issue of these Lundy stamps in 1955. The booklet *The "Puffin" Isle of Lundy*, published to accompany the 'Millenary Issue' of stamps, refers to, and is heavily influenced by, the Knights of the Black Raven in its section on the early history of Lundy.

No more is heard of the Order of the Black Raven, but MCH was always sympathetic to original and imaginative ideas.

The "Puffin" Isle of LUNDY

The 'Eric Bloodaxe' stamps, both denominated as 3 Puffin, one for surface mail and one for air mail

Death of Martin Coles Harman

O N SUNDAY 5 DECEMBER 1954, Martin Coles Harman died of a sudden heart attack at Godstone, Surrey, where he had just finished lunch at a hotel after one of his Sunday walks. On 16 December, Albion Harman brought his father's body for burial on the island. Taking the heavy coffin up the Beach Road was difficult, because a landslide had left a gaping hole across the path. However, it was manoeuvred across with care, and from there it was carried in the trailer, which was pulled slowly up to the plateau by the tractor.

The coffin of Martin Coles Harman being transferred from the 'Annie Vesta' to a dinghy in the Landing Bay

The dinghy and coffin arrive at the Landing Beach

The coffin is transported up the Beach Road on a trailer towed by the tractor

As is the island custom, all the islanders walked in slow procession behind the coffin, which was taken directly to the Beacon Hill burial ground, as MCH had not wished to have any church ceremony. There, in the cold still air, with the mourners gathered around, the Revd Muller read the burial service, and the coffin was interred beside the grave of Mrs Harman.

The funeral party arrives at Beacon Hill cemetery

The interment

Both graves are marked with boulders of granite so redolent of the character of the island itself, and each has a bronze plaque with the name engraved on it.

After tea at the hotel the funeral party boarded the *Annie Vesta* for their return journey, each with the sad knowledge that an era of Lundy had passed.

The graves of Martin Coles Harman (front) and his wife, Amy Ruth (behind). The square cairn at the rear is the grave of their second son, Albion Pennington Harman

Getting the builders in

AFTER the death of their father, Albion and his two sisters were determined to keep Lundy as they had known it. A major difficulty was the condition that the island was in. During the war maintenance had not been possible, due both to the lack of suitable labour and to the lack of building materials. A truly ferocious gale had occurred in 1944 that caused very serious damage to roofs and buildings that could not be remedied in war time, and many of them were in a sorry state. Diana takes up the story ...

'Aware of the potential value of Lundy's various buildings, however dilapidated, Albion set up a programme of restoration on a modest scale, so that visitors could stay, providing their own housekeeping, but with the full support of the island's resources.

'Albion was already fully committed to his well-boring business in Northern Nigeria, but with the help of his friend, Wimpey Worrow, a London architect, on their fleeting weekend visits to the island, plans for Castle Cottage were prepared. These were followed by plans for Hanmers, then the St Johns cottages, which did not require help from an architect. Ruth and I followed developments closely, and we were the furnishing team.

Left: the new walls of Castle Cottage swallow the old Cable Hut

Below: the view so enjoyed by stayers in Castle Cottage is framed

'Albion found the ideal local builder, Frank Rickard, to work the season on the restorations, bringing his mate, Charley Doherty, with him. Meanwhile a new generator shed was built, the Linhay was re-roofed, and new windows put in the Tavern. Later the Barton Cottages were rebuilt, with flat roofs, to house island staff, and the Austrians were the first to live there (see page 119).

Above: Wimpey Worrow and Albion Harman restoring the Linhay (Health & Safety inspectors look away now ...)

Right: Marion Harman Jones at Hanmers in 1962, with rebuilding work under way. A kitchen, a bunk bedroom, and a W.C. were built on at the back. Water was raised by a hand pump in the bunk bedroom and Calor gas was provided for the stove. It could sleep 2-4 people, is sheltered by its position in a cutting, and gives wonderful views of the east coast

'Following this, Frank Rickard was fully engaged with vital temporary treatment of dry rot in Millcombe. The copper roof was leaking, and a temporary flat roof was laid over it until a replacement would be affordable, which was later excellently carried out by Landmark. Ruth's and my views on furnishing were influenced by our past experience of musty cupboards, and damp and mildew in larders in the earlier style of houses such as Millcombe and the Manor Farm, and so we designed open shelves for the storage of crockery and pots and pans, making housekeeping much easier. Where possible lighter furniture was chosen so that housework was not a chore. In all the cottages, lighting and heating were by Calor gas. Fridges and hoovers were not available until Landmark came.

Above: the village, perhaps in the 1930s, when what is now Big St John's and Little St John's was a farm shed. Below: the modern view, with the Blue Bung to the right of the ever-popular St John's properties. Note the pitched roofs on Barton cottages, on the right, which are now flat

'The Blue Bungalow was not a letting property in our time. It was known as Albion's bungalow before Tubby Harrison took it over. In our days the Gades lived there in the summer and moved to Millcombe in the winter to keep the house aired, but Cheerful hated it when the move down came.

'In addition to Frank, Albion persuaded a local North Devon couple to make Lundy their home until their retirement. R.N. 'Dave' Davey and his wife, Chrys, joined the islanders as engineer and cottage carer. I managed the bookings from my home in Marlborough, and Chrys was the ideal person to care for the upkeep of the cottages and welfare of the tenants, who in many cases were old friends of Lundy. 'Dave' Davey was the vital and versatile man on maintenance, engineering, electricity and water resources. This was a brilliant appointment. Chrys was a popular sight with her donkey who carried the loads of linen and cleaning materials round the cottages, and it was a sad day when the poor creature died of bloat after over-indulging in some tempting fresh grass.'

Cattle, sheep and 'Pigs'

IANA continues the story ... 'Another introduction to increase income was a small herd of Galloway cattle, purchased with a loan from a friend, Tony Hatfield. Some Welsh sheep were also brought in to increase the flock, and although they were well suited to Lundy, they were not so easily handled and later were phased out.

'Then I set up the Tea Garden in the Pigs' Court – that was a major contribution in catering for the trippers that was set apart from the crowded Tavern, and at first I baked all the cakes that were served myself.

Left: the Pigs' Court before, in 1951

Below: the Pigs' Court after, in 1965

'The Hill Farm subsidy was the first grant that Lundy succumbed to. I remember feeling that it might indicate the beginning of the end of 'independence,' but Albion made a calculated decision that the need was more pressing than the threat of bureaucracy, which Lundy would always defeat through its inaccessibility. However, the net to include Lundy in paying income tax was circling and closing in since the fall of the Scilly Islands to inclusion with England.'

The *Lundy Gannet*

THE *LERINA* had been repurchased by Martin Coles Harman after she had finished her war work, but she had been neglected towards the end of the war and her condition had deteriorated. At Christmas 1947, she dragged her anchor while at Lundy and was damaged. Although repaired, she was never the same again and MCH decided to lay her up in 1950. She was sold in 1953 (see also page 27).

It was therefore a great event in June 1956 when the island had her own boat once again. The *Lundy Gannet* was so christened by Albion's son, John Harman, and her arrival was celebrated by a trip around the island to which many were invited; the weather was fine and the view of the island from the sea was a new and delightful experience. It had been intended that the boat should contribute to the island economy by fishing, though this did not materialise. But still, to have an island boat again was a most tremendous benefit.

The *Lundy Gannet* was Scottish-built and came to Lundy having originally been owned by a Bridlington fisherman – hence her Hull registration and her name, the *Pride of Bridlington*. It was originally intended to rename her the *Gannet* – Captain Dark's father had tended on Lundy for many years in his cutter named *Gannet* – but there was already a *Gannet* on the shipping register, and John Harman's bright idea of *Lundy Gannet* was the happy solution.

Kenneth Keast

DIANA remembers her husband and his part in Lundy life ... 'Ken and I were lucky to be able to spend his long school-master's holidays on Lundy. We would drive down to Bideford from Marlborough overnight in his old Rolls – usually fully loaded – to catch an early *Lundy Gannet* sailing. Ken was always happy on Lundy; from the earliest days in 1940, before we were married, he enjoyed every aspect of island life.

'After my father's death in 1954, Millcombe continued to be the shared Lundy home of Albion and Ruth's families and Ken and me. Ken always brought German literature with him – his preparation for another term – and his concentration seemed quite undisturbed by the hubbub of the house, whether from the 'Beatles' playing from a bedroom or a party up from the beach arriving in the hall with all the bathing paraphernalia to wash out and hang out over the terrace wall.

Ken and Diana at Millcombe

'Our Christmas holidays were usually spent in Alpbach, a village in the Austrian Tyrol, that Ken knew well. When full employment in Harold Wilson's Britain made it hard to find seasonal labour, Albion asked Ken if it were possible to bring some young Alpbachers to work the summer months on Lundy, so in 1961 the first young man, Hermann Lederer, gave it a try, and each year after that, he brought two or three friends with him. They were all farm people turned ski instructors for the winter, and the chance to learn good English on Lundy was a strong attraction. They were adaptable, skilful in building, sociable and very strong and agile. These arrangements continued for ten years.

'Ken greatly enjoyed clearing the slopes above Millcombe of brambles and bracken using an Austrian scythe which is smaller than an English one and ideal for steep pastures. In spring the daffodils and narcissi would appear unhindered on the cleared ground.

'On Lundy there is always much to do and Ken was a stalwart supporter with whatever was needed. On Campbell steamer days, the Tea Bar was set up, with Calor gas water boilers, tea urns, tables and crockery. I had started this for steamer days in 1956 and the cakes were made in Millcombe and had to be carried up in tins. When all was set up, it was only a short step to join the regulars in the Tavern from about 12.30 for a beer. Gi, Chrys and Dave Davey and Ken were the most reliable regulars on a daily habit which was one of Ken's most enjoyed moments of the day.

Ken, with Kay Harman, serving at the Tea Bar in 1960

'Ken's fondness for his old Rolls was rewarded in full measure, as it provided a means of transport for goods and furniture when Ruth and I fitted out each of the cottages in turn. Ken did many journeys from home to deliver a load to the *Gannet,* and on one occasion I packed 18 assorted chairs and stools to take down. Another time, three Victorian iron bar tables bought in Marlborough were transported – two of them are still in the Tavern today.'

DIANA SUFFERED a great loss in 1970 when Ken died of incurable cancer. Theirs had been a happy union, which grew from their meeting at Bedales School when Ken was teaching there and Diana was in her last year as a pupil.

It is usual to pay tribute to the qualities of one who has died, but in Ken's case it requires a long sheet of paper to describe him and the qualities that he brought to life. His academic career was grounded in the study of history, and by profession he was a teacher of languages (principally German). But the list is much longer: he was a cricketer, a musician, a singer of madrigals, a producer of plays, an actor, and a mover in many things that added enjoyment to life for those fortunate enough to share in them.

Two of Ken's talents were enjoyed on Lundy: he played the French horn, and occasionally his notes would be wafted down the valley from Millcombe. And his star turn in the bar was unforgettable: he had a deck chair, and would proceed to explain and demonstrate how it should be set up, despite the many wrong ways of going about it. He was calm and serious and it was hilarious.

Ken Keast in the cellar at Millcombe at the party to celebrate his and Diana's silver wedding

Family holidays: the next generation

In front of the Blue Bung in about 1955 are a mixture of Harmans and islanders. 'Podge' Russell (Kay Harman's sister) is on the left; the blond boy on the ground is Wayland Smith; on his left are Chris Russell and Chris Bull; Jack Evans (South Light) is on the side of the steps and 'Fee' (Dorothy) Caldwell, whom he married, is on the steps next to Kay Harman (far right). Between Fee and Kay are John and Inez Harman, and Marion and Martin Harman Jones are on Jack Evans' right

Above: Marion and Martin Harman Jones and John Harman

Right: Diana and Inez on the terrace at Millcombe

Above: shelling peas on Millcombe terrace in the late 1920s

Left: Young Martin Harman Jones with the skull and crossbones on the porch at Millcombe

Below: Albion at Millcombe

> *I remember at Millcombe rats looking down on us through a hole in the ceiling where a bell-pull used to be. On another occasion we were called upon by two Elder Brethren of Trinity House who had walked south after inspecting the North Light. We were sitting in the hall and I could see a rat run behind their sofa and out again along the skirting. To my relief they were unaware of this.*

Stanley Smith

STANLEY SMITH first came to Lundy in 1931 for a summer job from distressed South Wales and did so well in any work he was given that he was kept on the staff. Audrey Cannon, who was from his home town, came to Lundy to look after Mary Gade after she was born in 1933, and she and Stanley were married on Lundy in August 1938. Stanley had had a hard childhood and little opportunity for education, but he developed his intellect by assiduous reading under the guidance of a regular Lundy visitor who recognised and encouraged his potential. He developed a deep and passionate love for Lundy.

He continued to work on Lundy, and proved himself to be reliable, energetic and trustworthy in a number of roles until he was called up for the army on the outbreak of war. He used his time in the army to develop useful building skills that he was able to put to good use when he returned to Lundy with Audrey and their three children. The children insisted on choosing a Lundy name for themselves in addition to their given name: thus John Lundy Smith, June Lerina Smith and Wayland Pondsbury Smith.

Stanley's favourite book was Burton's *The Anatomy of Melancholy* and in his honour he constructed 'Burton's Seat', a monument between Benjamin's Chair and the Castle. In winter 1935-1936, he single-handedly excavated an emplacement just over the summit

Burton's Seat in 1936, not yet finished

of the ridge and brought dressed granite stones by wheelbarrow from as far away as Quarterwall Cottages with which he lined the work. Rene Gade declared the seat 'open and ready for occupation' at Easter 1936. Unfortunately, the Seat was destroyed after the war, when Mr and Mrs Gade were away, by an unknown person or persons.

Along with all his other jobs, Stanley took over as barman after Jim Prouse, when there were still no licensing hours and the barman worked for as long as people were drinking. In spring 1957, he published the first edition of his *Lundy Review*, which ran for six issues, and was a forerunner of the later and better known *Illustrated Lundy News*, with a mixture of history, news and reflections. Copies are now extremely rare.

The masthead of edition 3 of the 'Lundy Review'. The masthead reflected the 'home-made' nature of the publication and varied slightly with each issue

A postcard from 1957 showing the view from the Pigs' Court tea garden to the then white-washed Marisco Tavern. The chimney in the left-hand corner of the Tavern has now gone, and an extra window has been inserted in the gable end of what was then Marisco Cottage

A royal visit

A NOTABLE EVENT took place on 11 May 1958, when the royal yacht *Britannia* brought the Queen Mother for an informal visit to Lundy on her way back from a visit to Belfast. Great secrecy had been observed so that the press did not appear on the island (apart from two local reporters, told to keep it quiet, who were no doubt happy to have the scoop).

She was met on the Landing Beach and a tractor and trailer had been prepared with bales of hay covered with rugs. Felix Gade records in *My Life on Lundy* that when Albion asked the Queen Mother if she and her party would like to be driven up the hill, she replied, 'Oh no! I shall walk. You must not forget that I am a Scots woman, and can walk.'

She visited Millcombe, the Church and the Shop, where she bought postcards for her grandchildren, Prince Charles and Princess Anne. She was then entertained by the family to a picnic that was held near to the gate to Millcombe. On her departure she stood for people to take photographs, and was presented with a basket of fresh-caught fish, another of fresh lobsters, and two baskets of fresh herring gulls' eggs.

The Queen Mother and Ruth Harman Jones

Left to right: the Queen Mother, Peter Harman Jones, Lieutenant Colonel Sir Martin Gilliat KCVO, MBE (the Queen Mother's Private Secretary), Mrs Brodribb (with tray). 'Britannia' is visible in the background

The Queen Mother says goodbye. Albion and Ruth are on the right

The visit had been a success, of which Albion said that '... it was just like having a visit from a favourite aunt.' John Dyke had prepared a decorative parchment to commemorate the occasion, which the Queen Mother duly signed, and which remains on Lundy. So far as is known, it was a first ever visit to Lundy by royalty.

John Dyke's elegant commemorative parchment

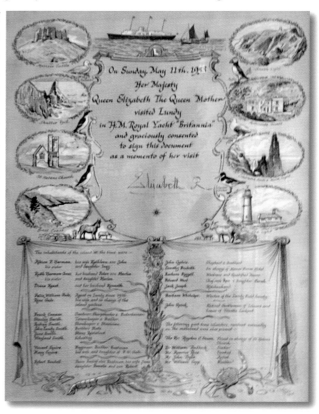

John Dyke

A PLACE LIKE LUNDY will sometimes attract an individual whose personal qualities are in particular harmony with it, to the extent that he or she becomes part and parcel of the island experience. Such a one was John Dyke. New arrivals would step off the boat or the plane and 'John's here!' would mean 'Good!'

John was born in 1923, in Denbighshire, and won a scholarship to Chester School of Art, where he was awarded both a gold medal and a prize for illustration. He worked for an agency until he was called up when war was declared in 1939, when he served in the camouflage unit. He made the maps for the invasion of Normandy and for the campaigns into Germany until the war ended in 1945.

After the war he worked freelance, and for a time this included artwork for the very popular comic, *The Eagle*. The family – by now with Joan, David and Jilly – moved to Devon to be near Lundy, which had already taken a strong hold on John's interest. He and Eddy Spiegelhalter set up the Atlantic Coast Studios, where many Lundy commissions were carried out.

John, Joan and Jilly Dyke at Signal Cottage in 1972

Renovations under way at Signal Cottages in August 1964

In 1970 John and his family were thrilled to move to Lundy, where he established the highly esteemed and popular *Illustrated Lundy News* (ILN). They lived in Signal Cottage South and were ever hospitable (jellies for the young), kind, and very popular. John was very witty and clever at making puns and amusing drawings, usually picking up some eccentricity – but always with good humour. He made cartoons of any event and, if one were extremely lucky, a hand-painted card would

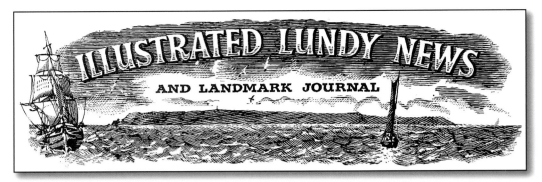

The masthead of the 'Illustrated Lundy News'. The name and the design style were a reference to 'The Illustrated London News'

arrive on a birthday, based on some idiosyncrasy of the recipient, or a recent notable happening. These were treasures, and never to be parted with.

This was not by any means the sum total of John's Lundy work; he drew some illustrated maps of the island (see, for example, page 5), and designed several issues of the Lundy stamps. Examples of his skilled work can be found throughout these pages.

John was interested in everything in, on, or round the island and was a fine raconteur and source of information. Happily he survived a heart attack in 1971, when he had to be airlifted to a hospital on the mainland and he couldn't get back to Lundy fast enough.

There was universal disappointment in 1975, when it was decided that the dearly loved ILN could no longer be afforded, so John and family had to go. Copies of the *Illustrated Lundy News* are now rare and treasured collectors' pieces.

John continued to work for the National Trust on the mainland. On Lundy he had been given the job of curator of items donated for the projected Lundy Museum. He took this collection with him to Cornwall but he was without any storage materials, space or any

John Dyke's drawing of his home on Lundy which he used as a letterhead for correspondence with subscribers to the ILN – for example, to encourage them to renew their subscriptions!

support. And though he took an interest in the items, and enjoyed reading some contributions, nothing was listed. John died in 2003; the collection was dispersed and the boxes and everything else were lost, although a very few copies had been made of some formal documents.

John and Joan Dyke's daughter, Jilly, worked on Lundy and married Reg Lo-vel, who was also on the Lundy staff and later became the Agent for a time. Jilly Lo-vel died tragically young, and a memorial plaque to her was placed on the Quarry Terrace in 1997.

Another example of John Dyke's detailed and beautiful work. This illustration was sold as a postcard. These days, the 'Fulmar Petrel' would be called simply a Fulmar, while the Buzzard – formerly a breeding resident – is now scarce on Lundy

Digging Lundy

LUNDY'S ARCHAEOLOGY is now well appreciated and monitored by the National Trust but it was not always so. In 1928, two visitors to the island, Mr Bristowe and Mr Lynex, asked for permission to excavate in Bulls Paradise. This was given in the hope that this would add to knowledge of island history. Unfortunately, although both were distinguished men in their own fields, they made use of picks and shovels to uncover two skeletons and a silver coin that was French, dated to 1380. Sadly the coin was never returned to Lundy and the one skull was smashed.

The first modern, scientific archaeological work on Lundy was done by Keith Gardner *(left)*, beginning in 1955. In the Lundy Field Society *Newsletter* for spring 2004, he recounts how, staying on Steep Holm with the then new Steep Holm Trust and discussing his great interest in islands and in archaeology, Harry Savory '... stretched out his arm, and, like Millais' *Boyhood of Raleigh*, pointed south west saying, "Then you must go to Lundy." There, he said, I would find a lifetime's archaeology that no one knew anything about. He wrote me an introduction to Felix Gade.'

The early work was surveying, photography and field-walking and the results were published in successive LFS Annual Reports. In 1962 Albion Harman gave Keith Gardner permission to excavate a site in Bulls Paradise, near the site of the so-called Giants' Graves. This burial was found *(below)*, dating from the fifteenth century, where the dead man had suffered a severe multiple fracture of the left leg.

A Bronze Age hut circle to the north of Gannets Combe, which is part of a complex of enclosures and huts that were laid bare, but unremarked, when severe fires destroyed the vegetation at the North End in the 1930s. The pole marks the doorway at the south east, and the remains of an enclosing wall can be seen. To sit inside this once-upon-a-time homestead, and ponder over the logistics of prehistoric home-keeping is no ordinary experience

Further digs were carried out during the Harmans' ownership in several parts of the island, and the work continued after the National Trust bought Lundy. Major excavations at Beacon Hill cemetery were directed by Professor Charles Thomas in 1969 where four early Christian gravestones had already been found, dating from the fifth to the eight centuries.

Two of Lundy's archaeological treasures. Left: the four early Christian grave markers, re-erected at the side of Beacon Hill cemetery. Right: a beautiful Bronze Age barbed and tanged arrowhead, found by chance at the North End by a visitor in 1970

In 1970, the Landmark Trust published Keith Gardner's indispensable *Lundy: an archaeological field guide*, dedicated to 'Harry Savory who sent me there and Albion Harman who received me'. In 2006, two years before he died, Keith Gardner privately published *An Archaeologist on Lundy*, his frank, witty and irreverent memoirs.

Diving makes its debut: a personal account

DON SHIERS remembers how diving began ... 'Diving on Lundy came about in 1966 following an invitation to me from Albion Harman to visit the island with a view to seeing if it would be of interest as a sport diving base, which if run commercially would be a means of generating an income for the island. I had met Albion in London in 1965 at the White House Club in Regents Park where we both were members.

'On this first visit I went across with Bill Bowen and Tony Matthews using one of my inshore rescue craft leaving from Bideford, while Albion Harman together with our respective wives and families travelled on the *Lundy Gannet* which also brought our diving equipment.

'Once on the island, having met Mr Gade and the islanders, we settled in to a week of diving at selected wreck sites under Albion's and Mr Gade's direction. This aroused my interest in salvaging some of the non-ferrous scrap from some of the wrecks.

Don Shiers (right) and Marten Webb of Bristol Channel Divers. Photo from the 'Illustrated Lundy News', Autumn 1971

'The following year I took a party of sport divers from The Aquatic Club based in London for some trial diving over a fortnight period to gauge their reaction. This turned out positive and encouraged me to open up a more permanent base on the island for the 1968 season and advertise to a wider diving audience. At the beginning of the season, with the help of the Austrians who worked for the island, we constructed a hut and store on the beach at the top end of the groin by Rat Island to serve as the base for diving operations.

'On 27 January 1969 Bristol Channel Divers Limited (name changed to B.C.D. Marine Limited in 1979) was formed with the intention of carrying out salvage in the Bristol Channel area. The first wreck purchased by the company was the *Amstelstroom* on 13 February 1969 which enabled us to begin salvage operations as well as running the sport diving centre.

'I had by now researched the history of the last known salvage company (Ilfracombe Coal and Salvage Company (1944) Ltd) to have worked the wrecks around the island and located the former shareholders – James Chenhalls, Laria Whear Chenhalls, Richard Thomas and John Thomas. I recall in 1968/69 meeting Mr Chenhalls at his house on The Quay, Ilfracombe, to view maple panelling which had been recovered from the *Montagu*'s wardroom which was put there by his father, James Chennells, the Managing Director of the Cornish Salvage Company Ltd (the initial salvors of the *Montagu* who purchased the wreck from the Admiralty). Then the Ilfracombe Coal and Salvage Company (1944) Ltd was formed with Mr G.H. Chenhalls as the Chairman. It acquired a number of the wrecks formally owned by the Cornish Salvage Co (1918) Ltd. However this company went into members' voluntary winding-up on 26 April 1947, with the shareholders maintaining an interest in the wreck assets.

'I made contact with John Thomas, who was the nominated spokesperson for the group and was living in France. Later Marten Webb and I went over to see him and negotiated a sale of the wreck assets which could be legally sold by the former shareholders of the company. A sale agreement was signed on 20 November 1972. The Lundy wrecks included in the sale were the *Montagu* and the *Carmine Filomena*. The last wreck purchased by the company was that of the *Robert*, on 25 July 1975.'

Images captured from 8mm film shot at Lundy mainly between 1966 and 1969 by Bill Bowen, John Shaw and Don Shiers

The Tavern

THE MARISCO TAVERN was the centre of island life in the Harman years as it is today. The bar could be just as crowded as it is now, with islanders, members of the Harman family and their friends, passing fishermen, ships' crews sheltering during bad weather and off-duty keepers from the lighthouses. These pictures give a feel of the old tavern, when it shared the building with the shop.

Right: this small porch was the one entrance to both the shop and the bar. The door to the bar was on the left and the door to the shop on the right. The original post box was fixed here after the G.P.O. was 'dismissed', and is being used here by Myrtle Langham in the early 1950s. Imagine the scrimmage on busy steamer days ...

Below: the shop in 1954. The ladies, left to right, are Cherry Richardson, Angela Garrard, Mary Squire (née Gade, with son, Peter), Mary Lea

Left: the bar in the 1950s. Jim Prouse is serving; Stanley Smith is nearest to him, then Felix Gade and Ruth Harman Jones. Jimmy George from the South Light is with his back to the camera and wearing a cap

Right: Leslie Harvey of the LFS at the dart board in 1954, with Frank Cannon looking on. The 'spotlight' provided by the candles looks a little vulnerable ...

Left: cabaret time in 1954. Most regulars had at least one party piece to entertain the company. Albion Harman's own very popular contribution was a song concerning a mother who lost her baby down the plughole

Above: the bar in 1966. John Ogilvie is propping up the wall, Arthur Strick is serving, Rene Gade is next right, and Chrys Davey is on the far right. The door behind Arthur leads to the shop

Right: Diana with Rear Admiral Keith Lawder in 1969. He was the first person to climb the Devil's Slide, which he did in 1961 at the age of 68

John Dyke painted a large mural of the bay on the south wall of the tavern, and pianists were warmly welcomed for the general entertainment. Space was always at a premium at busy times

A cosy winter evening in the bar. Wood for the fire was gathered by all from around the island. This is the bar before alteration but after 1980, because there is a lifebelt from the 'Kaaksburg' which was wrecked below Halfway Wall in November of that year

Albion Harman

I N 1966, BBC Wales made a 30-minute documentary about Lundy called *I have an island*. They followed Albion sailing from Bideford on the *Lundy Gannet* and interviewed him and many other islanders. In pieces to camera and in voice-overs, Albion spoke quietly and eloquently about Lundy:

Albion and Kay Harman. © Gordon Coward

I come to Lundy just as often as I can ... I've been coming here now since Christmas 1925 when I came for the first time as a small boy.

I like it. I love it. It is the one plot of land on all the earth that I really feel attracted to and like. I like it because living here is very difficult – sometimes one thinks in the winter time it's almost impossible. ... it seems to me that if one struggles hard enough and is ingenious enough in one's planning, that it *is* possible to live here in a self-supporting way. I don't mean self-supporting from the point of view of providing all ones own food, but for the island to be able to support itself – that is the thing that intrigues me, to build it up to enable it to do that – that is what I enjoy working on.

There are a great many people who fancy living on a small island away from it all, but they are mainly escapists, and in fact when they try it they don't succeed. What they really mean is they want to get away from the pressures and requirements of a more crowded life. They would like not to have to get up in the morning quite so early, not to have to work quite so hard, to be able to work when they fancy working – and of course life on an island is not like that. It needs, in fact, to be led successfully, even *more* self-discipline, even *more* determination, getting up even *earlier* in the morning, working even *longer* in the day.

People ask and wonder why one doesn't do more to commercialise the place and to turn it into a real thriving business. But that is not the aim that my sisters and I have for Lundy. If one made it into a bigger business one might make some money, but that is hardly everything, and certainly it would be a small reward for spoiling the very place that one loves.

Albion and Diana in 1965

Albion suffered a breakdown in health in 1967, and was on Lundy in June 1968 when he had a severe heart attack. He died in the helicopter which was taking him, with Kay, to hospital on the mainland. It was a devastating blow for the Harman family and a huge sadness.

A memorial fund was raised, and the LFS undertook the planting of some trees in Millcombe, which had been a particular interest of Albion's.

The memorial plaque to Albion Harman set above one of the benches in Millcombe

Lundy is sold

THE SAD TASK of selling the island fell to Albion Harman's wife and his two sisters. Without the capital resources to maintain it, or to repair a catastrophic landslip on the Beach Road which had happened in February 1969, there was no alternative. Lundy itself could never generate such sums as were needed. A sale was inevitable. It was a deeply sad moment.

Jack Hayward essentially 'saved' the island for the nation when he gave £150,000 in order for the National Trust to become the new owners, and John Smith of the Landmark Trust undertook a 60-year lease to administer the island and to restore the buildings, without which the National Trust could not have undertaken the ownership. On 29 September 1969, a new era began for Lundy.

This fortunate outcome was not reached before a period of worries, and some amusing diversions, had passed. One particularly engaging prospective purchaser was a Texan oil millionaire who was attracted by the idea of having an island of his own; he came with his family in their own plane, but he decided in the end not to buy. His decision was conveyed in a letter from Texas on the largest ever sheet of notepaper, in the largest envelope, with the largest typescript imaginable, that Mr Gade kept among his souvenirs.

Diana with Jack Hayward

Left: John Smith – later Sir John – the Chairman of the Landmark Trust with Jack Hayward on Lundy. Jack Hayward was also later knighted in recognition of his patriotic charitable works. As well as donating the money to enable the National Trust to buy Lundy, he also gave £150,000 for the return of the S.S. 'Great Britain' to Bristol and the same sum to the England Ladies' Cricket Team

Right: Peter Mills and David Owen, two of the West Country M.P.s who were concerned in the sale. Jeremy Thorpe, Liberal Party leader and M.P. for Barnstaple, led the campaign to 'save Lundy for the nation' and visited Lundy on several occasions

It is remarkable that Lundy devotees tend to have possessive feelings about the island, and strong ideas as to how it might be run – often to the annoyance of those whose job it was to try to make ends meet – while keeping it unspoiled.

In selling, the principle idea was that 'whoever takes over Lundy must love it as we do.' The three ladies were interviewed on the island by a reporter: 'Listen!' said Mrs Keast, and there was nothing to be heard but the bird calls and the sound of the sea. 'Where else today could you find such deep peace and tranquillity ... in so small a space? It is what we are determined will be preserved for posterity.'

Diana adds this postscript ... 'The sale to the National Trust had been concluded with profound relief and a sense of triumphant achievement by everyone involved.

'The months of 1969 had been a time of extraordinary effort by many friends and by the islanders who were understandably apprehensive of their uncertain future while being unstintingly supportive and helpful.

Some of the islanders in 1969. Seated, Felix and Rene Gade. Standing, left to right: Jane and Arthur Strick, Penny and John Ogilvie, Jean and John Stockwell, Chrys and 'Dave' Davey

'Conditions were not easy. The major collapse of the Beach Road in February, just before the sale was announced, had carried away Seaview, adding much time and effort to the man-handling of island supplies for months ahead. And in those days, normal contact with the mainland was either by radio transmitter via Hartland Point or by letter – weather permitting.

'I must record the names of the four able men who managed the business of the sale with such purpose and dedication:

- On Lundy, Felix W. Gade, the life-long friend, and agent for over forty years, who was host to the many prospective buyers and enquirers. His legendary letter-writing was at full stretch to deal with the volume of interest.

- In Barnstaple, Christopher M. Price, auctioneer and estate agent, who handled the sale. His knowledge of Lundy through his long friendship with Albion was a poignant force in his guidance and advice throughout his involvement.

- In Bristol, Clifton Smith-Cox was another good friend who gave professional help from his firm of accountants. He had developed a great affection for Lundy which grew from his chairmanship of P. & A. Campbell Ltd, whose paddle steamers sailed the Bristol Channel in summer.

- In London, Peter Harman Jones, representing the family, was above all the co-ordinator of events from the city office. He was a fully-trained lawyer and his own knowledge of the island set-up, its economy and personnel, reinforced Felix Gade's when facts and figures were needed from the island.

'Theirs was a great team indeed. They cared deeply for the welfare of Lundy and used their professional skills to achieve a triumphant result.'

Diana Keast after the service held on 26 September 2009 in St Helen's Church to mark the fortieth anniversary of the purchase of Lundy by the National Trust and its management by the Landmark Trust. The bouquet was presented to her at the end of the service by Derek Green, the Island Manager

Bibliography

Boundy, W.S., 1961, *Bushell & Harman of Lundy*

Catalogues of Sale: 1925, 1969

Gade, F.W., 1978, *My Life on Lundy* (2nd edition, 1997)

Gade, F.W., 1957, *The Postal History of Lundy*

Gade, M. and Harman, M., 1995, *Lundy's War*

Gardner, K.S., 2006, *An Archaeologist on Lundy*

Lundy Field Society, *Island Studies,* 1997

Lundy Field Society, *Annual Reports,* 1948-

Lundy Field Society, *Newsletters*, 1975-

National Geographic Magazine, May 1947, pp.675-698

Newman, Stanley, 1993, *Mailboats to Lundy*

Perry, R., *Lundy, Isle of Puffins*, 1940 (2nd edition, 1946)

Rendell, S. and J., 1999, *Lundy by Air*

Sack, J., 1959, *Report from Practically Nowhere* (reprinted 2000 by iUniverse.com)

Tedstone, M., 2001, *Lundy Packets*

Ternstrom, M., 2010, *Lords of Lundy*

Ternstrom, M., 'The Ownership by A.L. Christie, 1918-1925', *Lundy Field Society Annual Report,* 2006, pp.57-65

Webster, C. 'The origins & first 50 years of the Lundy Field Society', *Island Studies*, 1997 (Lundy Field Society)

Woodward, J.L., 2006, *A.T.V.B.*

Felix Gade. This drawing by John Dyke appears on the dust jacket of 'My Life on Lundy'